ROUGH JUSTICE

Memoirs of a Gangster

ROUGH JUSTICE

Memoirs of a Gangster

MAURICE 'BO BO' WARD
WITH JOHN MOONEY

MAVERICK HOUSE PUBLISHERS
Published by Maverick House,
Unit 115 Ashbourne Industrial Estate,
Ashbourne, Co. Meath.
info@maverickhouse.com
http://www.maverickhouse.com

ISBN 0 9542945 2 1

Printed and bound by AIT Nørhaven A/S, Denmark

The paper used in this book comes from wood pulp of managed forests. For every tree felled, at least one tree is planted, thereby renewing natural resources.

A CIP catalogue record for this book is available from the British Library.

For my children

Acknowledgements

I would like to thank a few people that were very important in my life. Firstly, my good friend Seanie Morrissey. You know what you mean to me. Thanks to my good friend, John Kelly, who restored my faith in people again. Victor Hackett has always been very good to me and I'd like to say thank you to him.

I would like to sincerely thank the gardaí in Bandon, Co. Cork who investigated my abuse claims, particularly Sergeant Gerard Crowley for the kindness, understanding and humanity he showed me.

Thanks to my family – my brothers and sisters. You probably have a fair idea about what will be in this book, but I hope you understand why I wrote it.

I'd also like to thank my counsellor, Muriel Moran, who changed my life.

Lobbins, you gave me a wonderful home for so many years and stuck by me through thick and thin. Thank you for your loyalty and for our children.

Lila, there are so many reasons I need to thank you and I don't say it often enough. Thank you for our boys and for your continued love all these years.

I'd also like to thank my children for all their love.

Bo Bo Ward

Acknowledgements

I'd like to thank a number of people for their help and support with this project. Firstly my friends Seán Curtin, Michael O'Toole and Paul Nicholls. Also to Darren Boyle and Anne Campbell who helped prepare the manuscript. Thanks also to Fiona Barry and Michael Kealey of William Fry Solicitors for their legal advice on various aspects of the manuscript. Thanks to Bo Bo's family and friends, particularly to Lila, his brother Tommy, his former wife Patricia and his daughter Linda.

John Mooney

Introduction

On the night of 28 April 2002, two masked men knocked at the front door of Maurice 'Bo Bo' Ward's home on Greenfort Avenue in Clondalkin, Dublin. When his partner Lila answered the door, one of the men forced his way into the house and walked into the kitchen where Bo Bo was having tea with his young sons.

The intruder was armed with a sawn-off shotgun. When Bo Bo saw his assassin coming, he remained calm and told the intruder he was in the wrong house.

The gunman did not respond but forced Bo Bo to his knees. He then lowered his gun and shot him at point blank range in front of his screaming children.

Bo Bo fell face down on the floor in a pool of blood. The killer stood over his body and fired another shot into his back before making his escape. A fighter to the end, Bo Bo struggled to remain conscious but his injuries were fatal. He died minutes later.

No one knows why he was killed or who was responsible. Theories abound to this day.

Some people think he was murdered by a local drug dealer who blamed him for the murder of Simon Doyle, a heroin pusher from Clondalkin. Bo Bo had kidnapped and threatened to murder Doyle for selling heroin to local youngsters.

Doyle died in a similar fashion to Bo Bo. He was shot in the chest after answering a knock on the front door of his home. He was also shot in the back as he lay on the ground.

But the truth is that no one knows the identity of the gunman or who ordered the murder.

It was always likely that Bo Bo would die a violent death. He was 56 years old and had been a criminal all his life. Ironically, just hours before he died, he had finished dictating this autobiography.

Bo Bo had begun writing the book in the autumn of 1999 while campaigning on behalf of child sex abuse victims. He had been physically and sexually abused in St. Patrick's Industrial School in Upton, Co. Cork.

By his own admission, he emerged from St. Patrick's a disturbed and violent young man who brutalised his wife and children. He also became a major player in Dublin's underworld.

Bo Bo sold heroin on behalf of the notorious Dunne family, he helped gangboss Martin Cahill to rob banks and also worked alongside Ireland's biggest criminal, John Gilligan. Anyone who crossed swords with him suffered the consequences.

His violent tendencies only subsided when he received professional help from a counsellor in the later years of his life. Those who knew him personally say he became a transformed character. You could say that he saw the error of his ways.

Writing *Rough Justice* was a depressing and heart breaking experience for him. When he examined his life in detail, he fell into a deep depression. He refused to forgive himself for the brutal beatings he administered to his wife, girlfriends and children.

His only wish was to make amends for the crimes he had committed.

I regret that he never got to see the publication of his book. I hope *Rough Justice* does him proud, but more importantly gives his children an insight into the man their father was.

Names that appear in italics have been changed to protect the privacy of the people involved.

John Mooney
June 2004

chapter one

Crime is the most addictive drug in the world. It consumes you. When you commit a crime for the first time, the feeling overwhelms you. There is no turning back. You never forget it. That rush of adrenaline pumping through your veins; it makes you feel invincible and drives you to commit more crimes. You develop an attitude; fuck the law and everyone else. You spend the rest of your life searching for that special feeling.

I know this now. Hindsight is a great thing but there was no talking to me all those years ago. And even if someone had tried to sit me down, I would not have listened. I would have told them to fuck off. That was my way of dealing with people. If I didn't like what I was hearing, I gave them a smack, kicked the shit out of them and burned down their house.

Sometimes I wonder would I have become a criminal if I had been born into a different background. Would things have been different?

I am middle aged now. I have fathered loads of children and made a mess of my life. I have been brutalised and tortured and I have brutalised and tortured others. I am a victim and an abuser in one.

To be honest, I don't want to write this book. I want to forget about what happened to me. I want to rewrite my life story. Start afresh as the posh people would say. If I could get a brain transplant to forget everything I would. I would give anything to start out again but I can't. It's funny, I spent my whole life telling lies to the gardaí and to my wife but now I'm trying to remember the truth that I desperately wanted to keep from everyone. That's the thing: there is only one truth.

I believe I became a robber to survive. Like most big time criminals, I was just a kid when it all started. A hungry, little, innocent kid, who took opportunities that landed at his feet because he had no choice. I could say the same about most of the gangsters that I befriended over the years. We all started out on the road to jail when we were still in short trousers.

The first time I robbed a shop was both the best and the worst experience of my life.

How could it be both, you might ask yourself? Well, I'll start at the beginning and see if I can explain along the way.

I was born in the Rotunda Hospital on 24 March 1946. My parents, just like any other young couple, were over the moon at the birth of their baby boy, or so they told me when I was a little older.

By the time I came along, my Ma and Da already had my older sister Mary though I was their third child. My older brother James had died of meningitis two years before I was born.

My father's name was Patrick and my mother was called Esther. They loved each other in their own way and did what they had to do to survive. In those days babies were not planned. They just arrived but my Da always told me that he loved me and wanted me.

When I was old enough to understand, he would sit me down and tell me about the day I was born. He used to say that he was on his way to the hospital to see Ma when I entered this world. I'll have you know that I had lots of black hair and blue eyes, just like my father.

Apparently he held me in his arms, kissed me and promised to never let any harm come to me.

That's what they told me when I was old enough to talk but I do think Da was delighted when I was born. You see, they were devastated when my older brother James died.

In those days it was survival of the fittest. The law of the jungle ruled because no one gave two shits about my people.

We were the poorest of the poor; we weren't even working class because my parents couldn't even find regular work. You get the picture.

We lived in one of the old tenements in Summerhill in Dublin's north inner city. There was only one room for us all – me, my sister Mary, and Ma and Da. It was a shit hole.

The only people who know the type of desperate poverty I'm talking about live in the poorest countries of the Third World. I'm not exaggerating; it was squalor.

The actual flat we lived in was over a bread and cake shop. A stairwell, which led down to a lane, joined all the flats together.

Our tenement was used as a toilet by the locals. When the men would fall out of the pubs at night, they would come into the lane and relieve themselves by urinating on the walls and on the ground. A lot of them did more than piss – they let everything out of their bodies. I will never forget the smell of that place. Can you imagine living in a building that people used as a toilet? The contrast between the beautiful smell of fresh bread and cakes mingled with piss and shit was overwhelming. I'm not kidding but I can still smell the piss and shit. It's lodged in my nostrils. It never went away. Even to this day I don't like using public toilets; it brings back too many old memories and smells that make me sick to my stomach.

But I suppose the smell of piss and shit made me immune to fear. Most people can't stand the sight of other peoples' shit, but I was forced to wade through it as a child. That made me strong although I didn't realise it until recently. When you can look at other peoples' shit, you can do anything. But it also made me want to get my own back on the world.

When I was a boy I harassed the people that used our stairs to piss and shit. There were old wooden rafters that hung over the lane. I used to climb up on the rafters and hide but I'd never play hide and seek. I got jam jars full of water and piss and when the women came into the lane to have a piss, I would be there in the rafters overhead and I would drown them.

It was my way of getting back at them for what they did every night. The people who lived in the tenements were forced to walk through their shit – you could not avoid it. That smell is the only memory I have retained of being a young child.

The smell of the bakery used to fuck me up. It was beautiful so you can imagine what it was like to go down the stairs smelling the bread and then having to walk into shit and piss and everything, because there'd be piles of shit everywhere along the lane.

To avoid it I always climbed out a window at the back of the flat and down a drainpipe across the waste ground, and out the side door that belonged to an old comic shop that was up to the left from us. That's why I was called Bo Bo. I could climb like a monkey down the drainpipe.

Going back to my life of crime; the first place I ever robbed was a cake shop. No prizes for guessing where. Yes, you're right; the cake shop under the flat. Remember what I said about being forced to rob? Let me explain what I mean.

There were three women and a man working in the shop and I used to go for messages for them. If they wanted butter, sugar or milk, whatever they wanted, I would go get it. My payment for going for the messages was a bag of crumbs. Now you might think I'm exaggerating when I say they paid me crumbs but that's what I used to get. Fucking bread crumbs!

They are all dead now but they were mean bastards. They didn't give a shit about starving kids and took advantage of me.

I was five-years-old when I got the idea to break in and take some food. It just came to me one day. For years afterwards I thought I broke into the shop because I was a natural born criminal, but I wasn't. I was a starving five-year-old boy. I was desperate and my family was poor.

The break-in was simple enough but I didn't think it through. I got in the back window of the shop one evening when they'd all gone home. As I crawled in the window, I had to drop onto the floor. Like all kids, I tried to fall on something soft. I knew there were barrels with flour in them near the window so I swung in that direction and landed in one of them. When I scrambled to my feet I was covered from head to toe in flour.

I will never forget that feeling of being terrified and excited at the same moment. The bread and the cakes were ready for the next morning. This was more food than I'd ever seen before. More food than my whole family had ever seen before. I filled up a flour sack I found under the counter with cakes and bread, had a look around and inspected the till.

Inside I found more money than I'd ever seen. There were farthings, half-pennies and three pence pieces, sixpenny pieces and even shillings. I can remember it as if it happened yesterday. I even remember being annoyed when I discovered there were no half-crowns. I pocketed the lot.

I then put as much cake and bread as I could carry into the sack and when I had everything ready, I sat on a stool beside the big cream cakes and ate as much as I could. I ate until I felt sick. Then I ate some more. When I was stuffed, I got my bag and made my way out the window. As I put the flour sack on my back, I peeped around the corner to see if anyone was in the lane.

You know what they say about the best-laid plans? When I looked out, the first thing I saw was two women having a slash in the lane. Fucking bastards. Now bear in mind I was covered in white flour from head to toe. I made a dash for the door to get to my Ma's room.

'Jesus, what was that?' said one of them.

'Something white just flew into the hall,' said the other one.

'Are you sure?'

I didn't hang around to find out exactly what they thought they saw. I headed up the stairs and left the bag in an old wash room across from our front door.

When the cakes were offside, I ran into our flat thinking that no one would be there. But when the door opened, I saw my Ma and her sister Mary.

'What in the name of Jesus happened to you? Come over here and let me see you.'

She hit me a box, pulled me in close and started brushing the flour off.

'Go into the wash room and take your clothes off before your Da comes home. He'll be here in a while. Get them fucking clothes off and I'll wash you,' said Ma. 'What the fuck happened to you?'

Figuring that I was going to be caught anyway, I told her I had a bag of cakes and bread that I had stolen from the shop downstairs. It was my way of telling her that I was trying to do some good by getting food for the family. I closed my eyes and waited for the slap but it never came. She just wanted to know if anyone had seen me.

The relief a child feels when they get away with doing something wrong is surreal. It was great. I thought she would hammer me.

I told her that two women had seen me but they didn't know what I was. She asked me what I was talking about before giving me a slap across the face.

'Where are the cakes and the bread?'

I went out the door and got the sack. I was running around without any clothes on and I looked like a freak.

It was a waste of time washing me. If you learn anything from this book, remember there's no point washing someone who's covered in flour from head to toe with water, because you just turn them into dough. Anyway I went into the washroom and brought the sack back into my Ma and Auntie Mary. They looked shocked but kind of happy. I knew they were happy but felt they couldn't show it – not to me anyway. I put the cakes and bread on the table. I laid them out in little piles.

'Put some of them in your bag Mary but don't tell Christy where you got them,' said my Ma.

This was great. I felt worthwhile. You know how young children like to please their parents. Adults forget that children will do anything to get genuine approval from their parents. Poor children are no different. We all want to perform for our parents; do things that make them happy.

'Ma?'

'What do you want?'

'I have money.'

'What?'

'I have money.'

'Where is it?'

'It's in my pocket in the washroom.'

The two women dragged me into the washroom. I picked up my shorts, put my hands into my pockets and handed Ma the coins. She walked back into the flat and started counting it. They sat down at the old table in the room looking at each other as if they had won the lottery.

'Is there any more money down there, Maurice?' asked Ma.

'I don't know.'

'Well get back in and see. Don't get anymore flour on you. I have no more clothes.'

That was a defining moment in my life. I knew what I was doing was wrong but my mother was telling me it was right. The feeling of exhilaration was gone. All I felt now was fear of being caught by the bakers or the gardaí. The second raid brought out different feelings. I was now scared.

I went back in and searched again. As if she knew, I found a few small bags with pennies, ha'pennys, shillings, two shilling pieces and that but no paper money. I was in the cake shop for a good while and then I heard, 'Bo Bo, where are you?'

'Here I am, here, look down here, I'm here.'

'Did you find any money?'

'Yeah, I found money.'

'Well get it and come out here and come straight up quick, there's no one in the lane and before you come out, get more bread.'

I filled up another bag of bread. I fleeced the place. I left nothing that I couldn't carry. I squashed more bread into that bag, let me tell you. I wrecked the bread. When I was done, I stuck my head out the window.

'Ma, are you there? Here, take the bag.'

I couldn't think straight because I was so nervous. Ma came down the stairs, grabbed the bag and flew straight back up the stairs. I crawled out the window and followed her into the flat. They were ecstatic. Auntie Mary was there with one of my cousins who had arrived to babysit me and my sister. Ma and Da were going to the pub with Auntie Mary and Christy.

Ma spread all the money on the table and began separating the coppers from the silver. She put the coppers in her bib pocket and told me that she would give them to Da. You could feel the sense of excitement in her voice. Auntie Mary was the same. They were over the moon. Ma was hatching and plotting how the money would be spent even though it wasn't hers. No one said anything to me even though I had done all the work.

Auntie Mary paced up and down the room. Then she told Ma to say she had got a loan of the money from her. I didn't care what they said. From my point of view, I couldn't get into trouble because Ma knew what I had done. I never found out what she did with the silver, but they went off to the pub that night as if all their dreams had come true.

When they came home that night they were drunk and singing. Ma came over to me and lifted me up.

'How's my little man?'

She pulled me close to her and I could feel the warmth of her breath and the smell of drink. Da was there with Christy and Auntie Mary. He lifted me into his arms, gave me a hug, then handed me to his brother.

My mother grabbed me again. She looked at me, winked and smiled, putting her hands on my cheeks, pulling my head on to her shoulder. She held me close in her arms beside the window, which overlooked Summerhill.

I loved sitting on my Ma's lap. It was heaven. I felt loved and important. I remember her rocking back and forth and humming to herself. I cuddled into her shoulder and closed my eyes. I loved to see my mother happy. I would have done anything for my mother.

I remember her singing that old song 'See how the harbour lights are shining' into my ear. I never experienced that sort of feeling with any other woman.

When I woke up the next morning, Ma told me the gardaí were down at the shop. She sat me down at the table and gave me a big lump of bread with margarine and jam. This was something we didn't have often.

'Do you remember you told me there were two women in the laneway when you came in with the cakes and bread yesterday, Bo Bo?'

'Yes.'

'When me and Mary were in the pub, this aul one came out of the toilet and said she saw a ghost in the lane.

'She swore they saw an angel walking into the flat. A pure, white, little angel.'

I didn't get the story. I was more worried about the gardaí and what would happen if someone had seen me. That was the only thing on my mind. Anyone who has ever robbed will tell you that that's all they think about for days after a job.

'A ghost Ma?'

'Not a ghost, you fucking eejit. They saw you. They thought it was probably your little brother Jimmy, the light of heaven to him. They said Jimmy needs the family to say prayers for him. They said he is in limbo and we had to pray for the children. They think you were an angel – some angel.'

I never wanted anything but love from my Ma. She gave me love when I provided for her. I looked upon robbing the cake shop in the same way as children look at getting good marks in their exams. I had done something good; something that my Ma could be proud of. That particular belief vanished within minutes when she started thinking about the gardaí. That unnerved her.

When I finished the bread, she dragged me over to the sink to wash my face. When she tried to comb my hair, the comb broke.

'What in God's name am I going to do with you? Now you listen to me. You stay away from the cake shop today and don't let anyone see your head or they'll all know you were in the shop.'

The cake shop did not open that day. I remember I got some money from Ma and went to Tara Street baths with a big bar of carbolic soap. I came home sparkling like a little angel.

I wasn't worried about the flour in my hair. I couldn't have cared less; I scrubbed myself clean to get rid of the evidence. I was only five-years-old but I was already learning the tricks of the crime trade.

chapter two

For the first few years of my life things were difficult, then when I was about six-years-old, we moved to a flat on Gardiner Street. Our new home was located around the corner from the old tenement building. I had no difficulty at all with the move. I was overjoyed at the thought of not smelling other peoples' shit when I woke every morning.

Our new home had two rooms. To a boy from the tenements, it was heaven. The working class people who lived on Gardiner Street were a hardworking lot who kept to themselves and went about their daily business.

I remember the day we moved as if it happened yesterday. Ma and Da were excited for weeks packing away what few belongings we had. We might as well have been moving into a four star hotel. Ma was in a fluster for weeks. She couldn't stop talking about our new home. I think Da was excited because there would be two rooms, which would give them some privacy in a tiny flat overrun with children. The more I think about it now, the more I realise how suited my parents were. They balanced each other. Da stopped Ma getting ahead of herself while Ma encouraged Da to want more from life. They were good together.

The family didn't stay long in Gardiner Street because we were offered a more spacious flat on Sean McDermott Street. I always thought it funny that my family moved three times when I was a child but stayed within 100 yards of the place I was born. I suppose the people of the inner city don't like straying too far from home. They like the places they know the best and being surrounded by their extended families and cousins. I suppose my parents were no different.

I never really felt that kinship with the city because of my thieving. I grew to learn that being known to everyone has its disadvantages. It is not a good thing when you are a criminal. People are often too willing to identify you to gardaí.

The move to Sean McDermott Street came as I started attending Rutland Street School. I didn't like the lessons but I loved the discipline and the kids. School was great. It was the best time of my life. The boys just wanted to play and run riot all day long. Young boys tend to congregate in gangs and we were no different. I was delighted with the sense of kinship that came naturally to us all. We were obviously not a criminal gang because we were just seven-year-olds but we had a wild streak about us. We were rough and ready. We were tough boys, street urchins, call us what you like. I suppose you would say we were out of control. Well that's true. Of course I now realise that I was out of control but at that time I saw myself as just having a lot of freedom. That is, freedom to rob.

My gang, if you can call them that, started off robbing orchards, which was the height of sophisticated crime to a gang of seven-year-olds from the city. Every day, we would meet in an alleyway off Gardiner Street where there was an old mill house. After some small talk, we would go our separate ways in twos and threes and head out to places like Clontarf to rob orchards.

Most youngsters do this type of thing at sometime in their life but they stop when they get caught. Anyone who tells you that they haven't robbed an orchard is a liar.

My biggest problem was that no one caught me because I was too good. At least that's what I believed.

Although I was rough and ready, I was never the sort of person who would fight people just because I didn't like the look of them or rob old people. That came later.

At that stage I was just a bit of a wayward boy who was always on the lookout for an opportunity. I would be lying if I said I continued to steal to feed myself. I did rob the cake shop in Summerhill because I was desperate for food but I continued thieving simply because I could. You might recall that I said crime is like a drug. It is. When I got away with the cake shop job, I began to look at the world in a different way. I tuned my senses to thievery.

I would watch out for unlocked doors, opened windows and ways of entering shops to rob anything that was valuable. I stole because I could and for sheer excitement.

I changed in those years. Few people realise that children who get involved in petty crime are different to ordinary kids. They eventually come to trust no one because they themselves cannot be trusted. In simple English, you apply your own standards and values to everyone else. Not alone would I clean out a shop of all its valuables, but if the chance presented itself, I would also rip off the boys who robbed with me.

Don't get me wrong. They would do the same to me; we expected it of each other. The only thing that bonded us together was the fact that we knew we couldn't trust each other.

Let me tell you a story of one particular place I robbed at the time. It was a supermarket on Parnell

Street, a busy shopping area close to my home. The street was always full of shoppers and market traders. The biggest shop in those days was a supermarket called Liptons.

I remember walking along Parnell Street with two of my friends and looking in Liptons' window. Through the corner of my eye I noticed a brass plate with the word 'Mail' engraved on it. This was for deliveries.

I took a closer look at the parcel box and reached up to see just how big the opening was. When I flipped the lid, I reckoned I could get my head into it. As far as I was concerned, this was an opportunity not to be missed. I told the two kids that were with me I would crawl into the parcel box and open the back door for them, if they lifted me up. The back door of Liptons led out to a place called Cow Lane.

'Don't be so fucking stupid,' said one of the kids. 'You'll never get your head in there, Bo Bo.'

'If I can get my head in, I can get my body in.'

The little fucker with me that day was a real doubting Thomas. He objected to everything I did. He was always the same. I had proved him wrong several times that week.

He had said I wouldn't be able to open the back door of the cinema to let the boys bunk in but I did. So I told him to fuck off and go home. I said I was off to get someone who was not afraid, which unfortunately prompted him to give me a dig in the mouth before he ran off.

The other kid had more faith in my abilities and stayed with me. I told him to put his back to the mail plate and lace his fingers together. With that I went up and in head first.

The shop was closed and there were no security guards in those days, which left me free to my own devices. I was fearless.

I opened the front window and told my accomplice to go round to the back door on Cow Lane. I said I would open the door.

But that was a ploy. I went straight to the cash tills to steal the lion's share of the proceeds; after all, I had taken all the risks.

Liptons was like any supermarket. The tills were located near the front door exits. There were two tills on one side of the shop, and two tills on the other. The first till I inspected had a few 10 shilling notes. I stuffed them in my pockets. I did the same with the others.

The golden rule in thieving is making sure not to leave anything behind. When I emptied each till, I searched for cash boxes and safes that might contain more money. When I was cleaning out the last till, I found a cash box under the desk that was full of £1 notes. This was big money as far as I was concerned. I didn't have time to count the money so I hid the notes in my shoes and in my pockets. If I got caught, the gardaí would search my pockets but they would never think of my shoes. I never touched the silver or the pennies. I left them for my partner who was still waiting at the back door. When I had taken all the cash, I made my way to the back door to let him in.

Liptons was like Aladdin's Cave. It was December so all the turkeys and Christmas cakes were on display. We went straight to the tills where we found some change. We shared the silver between us. I never told him about the paper money, which was the real loot.

After having a good look around, we decided to take everything. When I say everything, I mean everything we could carry; the turkeys, cakes, chickens, rashers, sausages, black and white puddings, sweets, tea and sugar.

I rummaged around the shop looking for big brown paper bags to carry our load. But, of course, being kids, we filled up bags that we couldn't carry. It was too late by the time we realised our mistake.

But fortune was on our side that particular evening. Luck would have it that there were a couple of prams left by the market dealers in Cow Lane.

Liptons were well liked by the locals in the north inner city and the manager obliged the traders by letting them leave their prams at the back door.

The two of us got a pram each and loaded the bags into them before escaping. We made no attempt to disguise what we had done. We left the backdoor swinging wide open and headed off in the general direction of home with a week's shopping.

No one said a word to me. People walking along the street didn't even notice. When I reached our flat on Gardiner Street, I emptied my loot into an old coal-bunker and headed back up to load up once more. When I got to Cow Lane, I saw a few kids standing around the back door. Word of the break-in had spread fast. The best way of dealing with a situation like this is to attack first. So I said, 'What the fuck do you want?'

'We can take whatever we like. You don't fucking own this place, Bo Bo.'

They had a point so I pushed them aside and filled the pram up again. I stole a big turkey and a few puddings. I deposited the second load in the bunker and was on my way back for a third load when I saw the gardaí from a distance.

The kids used to call them the Rossers. There were two of them in black uniforms and they had two of the kids who, from a distance, looked as if they were bawling their eyes out crying.

Crime is all about self-preservation. The pram was dumped on the spot and I headed straight home. When I was safe inside the flat, I opened the front window and looked out to see if the Rossers were searching for me. I couldn't see anything suspicious on the street, which was a good sign.

Ma came home about 30 minutes later. She had been down in Henry Street selling flowers to try and get a few bob for Christmas.

It was time to come clean. I told her what I had done and when I opened the coal-bunker, boxes of biscuits, turkeys, sugar, butter and everything that she could possibly have wanted, fell out.

Ma was delighted but she would not show it. She had nothing to cook for Christmas that year so I was the hero once again. That made me feel worthwhile. I vividly remember that my mother was genuinely grateful for what I had done but I sensed that she felt regret for not punishing me. This was not the life she wanted for her boy but she had no choice. Our circumstances had seen to that.

She sold some of the food to her brother Johnny, who lived upstairs, and she sold some to Auntie Mary.

Even as a child I knew my family was in serious financial difficulties. That's why I gave her the money I stole. Perhaps this is why tears came to her eyes when I handed her fistfuls of cash.

I remember she hugged me for ages that night and told me not to say a word to anyone, especially not to my father. He was the type of man that no matter how hard life had become, he would never permit his children to break the law.

Ma knew the reality of life. In the years since, I have come to realise that Ma accepted my errant ways in the misguided belief that I would somehow become a reformed character when I grew older. Rather than punish me for theft, she ignored what I was doing and rewarded me. I suppose she felt she had no other choice.

I can't remember how much money I stole from Liptons but there must have been a nice few quid in it. When Santa visited our home that Christmas, I got a horse and trailer. I was also the best-fed boy in Sean McDermott Street.

I always viewed the Rossers as a sleeping tiger waiting to pounce. Criminals have to be lucky the whole time, the police only have to get lucky once and you're nabbed.

My first brush with the law happened not long after the Liptons robbery. It was on the cards but I did not see it that way. When you engage in any form of criminality, you convince yourself that you are smarter than the gardaí and cannot be caught. This may seem foolhardy but you have no choice. If a robber sat down and thought about the reality of what they were doing, they wouldn't venture out of the house. Criminals have to convince themselves they are unstoppable in order to commit crimes but it is impossible to get away with crime forever. Sooner or later you get caught. I'm not saying you go to jail the first time, or even get charged, but you always get caught. What happens afterwards is largely down to the way you handle the situation.

Do you remember what I said about opportunities presenting themselves when you least expect them? I was walking along Marlborough Street near my home one afternoon and I saw a breadvan pull up outside one of the shops. The breadman began unloading the van, lifting trays of bread and cakes. When he went into the shop, I walked up to the driver's door and looked in the window. This was an opportunistic theft. I opened the van door and started searching the cab. Underneath the driver's seat I found a moneybag. It was a leather bag with a strap.

I had robbed delivery men before, so I knew the bag contained decent money. I grabbed the bag and ran off making my way to Sean McDermott Street. In those days, the big houses had underground basements that were left vacant, so I headed into one of these and started counting the money. I pocketed the lot and was about to leave when a little girl from the area named Bríde came down to the basement.

'Hello, Bo Bo. Are you not in school?'

Bríde was a lovely little girl. You know the sort; she was as sweet as pie and totally innocent but a nuisance.

I told her I was sick and that I couldn't go to school. In fact, I went further, saying my Da wouldn't let me go to school because I was so sick.

'What's in the bag, Bo Bo?'

I was caught on the hop. I did the one thing that I normally never did. I handed Bríde the bag and told her to keep it. I gave the evidence to someone who could implicate me. I still don't know why I did it.

Bríde went off delighted. I went upstairs asking why I didn't just tell her to piss off. I went to the front window of our flat, because if anyone came into the street you could see them coming from our front window. Usually when anything was robbed around Parnell Street, the owners headed down to Sean McDermott Street to see if they could catch the kids.

For some reason I felt certain that trouble was coming and I was right.

At that moment, the breadman came around the corner with Bríde by the arm. Worse again, Bríde was pointing up at the window where I was looking out. I looked back in absolute shock. I looked straight into the breadman's eyes with guilt written all over my face. I was fucked.

The only course of action open to me was to deny everything. I jumped into bed and pretended to be asleep.

I don't think I could have felt worse if I'd been beheaded. Just when I thought things couldn't get worse, Ma and Da came in.

'What are you doing in bed?'

Even now I remember that moment as if the scene is permanently etched into my memory. I recall Ma looking at me in puzzlement while Da knew straight away that I had done something wrong. He had that way about him.

I decided to stick to my story because I had no alternative. Pulling myself out of bed, I looked them straight in the eye and told them I'd been in bed all morning.

Then I heard a knock on the door. Da stared at me while Ma went out and answered the door. Da never broke eye contact with me. He knew I had been up to no good. He just kept staring at me. Ma called Da to the door. Da summoned me out of bed a minute later.

'Bo Bo. Come here now!'

'Yes, Da.'

'Come out here! Did you give this bag to Bríde?'

He held out the leather bag I had stolen. My world was about to cave in. I felt like getting sick. I was caught red-handed. I decided there and then that I had two options. If I admitted to stealing the bag, I was dead. Da would have leathered me.

I also knew there was no point in denying that I gave the bag to Bríde. Why would she tell lies about me, and she was no thief. I kept asking myself why I gave the bag to her. I cursed the ground she walked on.

There was only one thing to do; stick to the story.

'Yes Da. I gave the bag to Bríde.'

'Where did you get it?'

'Downstairs Da, at the back of the hall.'

Da knew I was lying but the breadman wasn't so sure. He asked me if there was any money in it.

'No, sir.'

'Are you satisfied?' roared Da. 'He found it down the back of the hall and he gave it to her. Well, what's your problem?'

Da stood his ground. In that moment I felt guilt. Da was defending me because I was his boy and he believed me above anyone else. I felt proud of him and ashamed of myself. There were many things I didn't know at the time but I had learned the importance of family and kinship. I wanted to admit what I'd done to save Da any embarrassment but I couldn't, which made matters worse. The breadman had no option but to call the gardaí. The minute he mentioned the gardaí, Da flipped.

'Well get them. Now fuck off away from the door and don't come back,' roared Da slamming the door shut.

I turned to walk away but Da grabbed me.

'Did you rob that man's bag, Bo Bo? Just tell me the truth.'

'No Da, I didn't. I swear to God I didn't.'

'If he brings the police up here, I'll kill you. You know what will happen if you tell lies.'

He pointed to a brown leather belt around his waist. I was terrified. I actually prayed to God to intervene. I said about three prayers in the space of a minute. The next thing I heard was footsteps approaching our front door.

It was the the breadman with two gardaí. I was terrified. I tried to listen as best I could to the conversation but all I could hear were the adults arguing.

'Bo Bo, come out here now,' roared my Da.

'Did you take that bag out of that man's van?'

'No, Da. I found it at the back of the hall. I swear to God, I found it at the back of the hall. I didn't touch it.

'When I found it, there was nothing in it. It was empty, I swear to God, Da. I gave it to the little girl; she said she wanted it and I gave it to her.'

The two Rossers stared at me. They knew I was lying. Gardaí might have the personality of water rats but that doesn't make them stupid. Anyone with a brain cell knows bad liars always embellish their stories by adding extra details to make it more convincing. A good liar will say nothing. He will give away no specific information unless asked and won't say anything he cannot prove.

'Where did you say you found it?' asked one of the gardaí.

'At the back of the hall, just at the back door.'

I made a point of making direct eye contact with him to try convince him of my innocence.

'You found it at the back of the hall?'

'Yes sir, I found it at the back of the hall, just at the back door and I was playing with it down in the area, and Bríde came in and she asked me for it and it was no good to me, so I gave it to her.'

Rossers work on hard facts. Whether they believed my story or not was irrelevant. They had no proof. They had no option but to go away and drop the matter.

I hoped the episode had ended right there and then but no sooner had the gardaí and the breadman left than Da turned to me and said, 'If I find out that you took that man's bag, I'm telling you.'

He didn't say another word. He just pointed at his belt. He was content to let the matter rest. I kept up the pretense that I was sick.

The atmosphere in the flat slowly returned to normal. Da asked me if I wanted to go to the shops with him but I said I didn't feel well, so off he went.

Ma grabbed me the moment he walked out the door.

'Now tell me the truth, Bo Bo. Every time you tell a lie you bite your jumper. Now tell me the truth or I'll fucking kill you. Did you take the money?'

'I did take it and I hid the money.'

'Where is it?'

'It's on the roof.'

'Go up on the roof and get the money and I won't tell your father. I won't tell your Da. I have to get milk and bread, so get up on the roof and get it, and leave it here for me for when I get back.'

I did as I was told. I had hidden the cash under some planks of wood. As much as I am ashamed to say, I didn't even trust my own mother by this time. I had become twisted. I wanted some money for myself though I'm not sure why. I kept some of the coins. I came back downstairs and began counting the rest when I heard someone at the door. I presumed it was Ma and paid no attention.

It was my Ma but my Da was with her. He turned red when he saw the money and lashed out.

All I remember is getting a bang on my right ear and landing on the floor. I sat there with the buzz in my ear stinging me. Da was going for me again but Ma saved me.

'Leave him alone. Take some of the money and go for a pint. Go on.'

Of course Da was furious. He wanted to kill me. I don't think he was angry because I had stolen the bag. All the boys of my age were doing the same thing. He was upset because he had attacked the breadman. Da knew right from wrong. He knew he should have trusted his gut feelings but his loyalty to me had let him down.

He walked over to the table, took some of the money, and walked out the door. I never moved from the floor. He never even looked in my direction; I just sat there with a ringing sound in my ears.

Ma walked over to me, leaned over and scooped me into her arms. She gave me a hug.

'You will get yourself killed, Bo Bo, if you keep this up. I won't be able to help you. If you don't stop, you'll be taken away. Are you listening to me, Bo Bo? Your day is coming.'

chapter three

By the time I reached ten years of age, I had abandoned my school studies for petty crime and thieving. I spent most of my time hiding from my teachers and running wild around the streets of the city. Even when I attended school I didn't listen to anything the teachers had to say. Homework was out of the question.

I lived a carefree life. I didn't care for anyone or anything. I was afraid of no one. I often think back and ask myself what drove me to hate school considering I liked it at first. I honestly can't answer that question. I love reading books now and watching documentary films on wildlife but back then I had no interest in anything other than thieving and mitching. Trouble always found me and when it didn't, I went looking for it. From my point of view, school was something that just got in the way of thieving and making money so I mitched classes. I thought no one would miss me when I was gone, which seems ridiculous now.

I didn't know it at the time but my carefree lifestyle and constant thieving was about to change the course of my life forever.

In the second week of January 1957, I was brought before the Children's Court. Da had been convicted twice for my non-attendance in school. I had also been caught stealing a bible from a priest's car in Marlborough Street. It was another opportunistic theft. I was walking by the car when I noticed a pound note sticking out of a bible on the passenger seat. So I said to myself, whoever left that there deserves to be robbed. The opportunity was too much to resist, but I got caught red-handed.

Some official had come to our house and told Ma and Da that I was being prosecuted. I can't remember if Ma tried to explain what was happening but I recall her taking me to the Children's Court, which was located on Castle Street. I'll never forget that day. It changed my life forever.

I was only ten-years-old and I didn't really see myself as anything other than a young boy. But my view of myself changed that morning when Ma brought me to court.

When we arrived at the court there were loads of people hanging around outside. There were five kids who looked scared. I knew I was in trouble.

I stood there with Ma for half-an-hour when I heard my name being called.

'Ward, send up Ward.'

I remember Ma kissed me on the head and sent me over to a Rosser waiting at the door.

'Come on! Come on! The judge is waiting.'

'I'm waiting on my Ma.'

'Your Ma will be up in a minute; go on up there into the room on the second floor.'

I walked up a flight of stairs and into the courtroom. It was a big room and I was directed to stand beside a Rosser. My name was called out.

'Maurice Ward. Come forward please.'

'I'm waiting on me Ma.'

'Your Ma will be up in a minute.'

I was now standing in front of the judge. His name was Mr. District Justice McCarthy. He was a stern looking man who frightened the crap out of me. He began to ask questions to some bloke in a pinstripe suit and another Rosser who I'd never seen before.

The whole thing lasted no more than a few minutes. I didn't listen to what they were saying but I heard the judge sentencing me to six years in some place called Upton. I froze on the spot. Six years in Upton!

What the fuck is Upton?

The Rosser took me by the arm. I thought he was bringing me out to my Ma, who was standing at the back of the court. But he didn't. Ma was in floods of tears. The Rosser walked me straight past her and brought me downstairs to a holding cell under the stairs of the courts.

'Where's me Ma? I want me Ma. Is this Upton?'

The Rosser locked me in the room and told me he would go out and bring her to me. There were a few kids in the cell. They were all crying and so were their mothers and fathers. I sat on the left-hand side of the room on my own. There was a boy from the corporation buildings sitting there with his big sister. I knew them and asked them what the fuck was going on.

'What happened to you, Bo Bo?'

'I don't know.'

'You must have been sent away. Otherwise you wouldn't be in here. You're fucked now, Bo Bo.'

'I don't know.'

'Is there anyone with you?'

'Me Ma's outside. The Rosser said he would bring me Ma in here now to sort this out.'

I was shitting myself. Where was me Ma? Six bleeding years in Upton. I couldn't plan ahead for six minutes.

I was locked in there for a good while. I began to panic. Where was Ma? What the fuck was going on? I asked the girl to knock on the door and ask the Rosser about me Ma.

The girl was going out to the shop to get her brother a few sweets. She told me that her brother had been sent to Artane for five years. The Rosser came down a few minutes later. He said he was talking to my Ma but that she had gone home.

I told him to stop lying and get me Ma. I knew he wasn't lying so I did the only thing I could. I went fucking mad. I started screaming and shouting. How could she do that to me?

The Rosser told me to calm down, then he explained that I had been sentenced to six years. I freaked; I panicked and began crying. I started screaming the house down.

I will never forget that Rosser. The guy felt sorry for me. He put his arms around me and told me I would be all right. I often attacked gardaí in later years but I will remember that man's kindness 'till the day I die.

He knew the score and did what he could for me. The rest of the people took pity on me at once. One of the mothers came over to me and gave me sweets but I couldn't even put them in my mouth. I was crying uncontrollably. I didn't know what to do. After a time the mothers left the holding room and we were taken away.

I was the only one sentenced to Upton in Cork. The rest were going to places in Galway and Dublin. A car came to take some of us away – three of us to a place in Glasnevin. I will always remember the car used to transport us. It was big and had a wooden interior. It was the first time I'd been inside a big car.

When we reached Glasnevin, all our belongings were taken from us and put into a bag. I kind of said to myself, this isn't too bad Bo Bo. But was I wrong or what?

'Maurice Ward?'

'Yes.'

'You call me sir, do you hear that?'

'Yes, sir.'

'You were sentenced to Upton in Cork for six years, we will hold you here 'till you are transferred to Cork. Go over there and sit down and I will deal with these boys.'

I was afraid to ask any questions, but I was especially afraid to ask the question that haunted me: when were Ma and Da going to arrive and sort this out? When the man was finished filling out some paperwork and processing us, he ordered us to follow him.

He brought us into a big room where there were about 15 kids already waiting. Some of them were crying while the others were letting on they didn't give a fuck. But we were all scared.

I sat down and one of the kids came over and asked me if I had any cigarettes. I didn't smoke. The boy then asked if the other kids had any.

The man at the counter overheard the word 'smoke' and he flung a packet in the air. All the boys dived on me and fought for the cigarettes. What kind of a place was this? It was like a jungle.

I didn't know what was happening. I was very confused and frightened. We were given cocoa and bread for tea before we went to bed. I don't remember much about the few days I spent in Glasnevin, but there is one thing that sticks in my mind. There was this kid there, we used to call him 'Boots'. Apparently his father knew a lot of the men that worked in there. But this kid had these hobnailed boots and he'd always kick you. He'd kick you for nothing. When he tried to kick me, I gave him a belt in the face and he didn't do it again.

I spent about three days in Glasnevin before I was moved to Upton. The warders told me the night before I left Dublin that I would be leaving early the next morning. I was woken up by a warder at 5.00 a.m. The bastard pinched my arm, which left a mark on my skin.

'Get washed and dressed, and come downstairs. I'll have something ready for you to eat when you come down.'

I did as I was told. As I went down to get my clothes, I decided my own clothes were shabby so I'd take someone else's. That fucker Boots had left his hobnails and stockings at the end of the bed so I robbed them. I nicked someone else's trousers, someone else's jumper and some boy's shirt.

I figured by the time they discovered their clothes were missing, it would be too late. I would be on the train to Cork.

Off I went with my new clothes to have my sup of tea and a bit of bread. When I was finished, I was told the police were outside waiting on me. I acted like I didn't care. Wherever this Upton place was, I was going to run wild. That's what I kept saying to myself.

The Rossers drove me to Kingsbridge station where I was handed over to two Rosminian brothers. They introduced themselves to me. They seemed nice enough and I did as they said. I would have no problem running rings around these fellas. I was going to be okay. Fuck my family. Who cared anyway, I said to myself. This was all bravado, of course. I was terrified.

As the brothers were talking to me, I heard a familiar voice. It was my Da.

'Bo Bo! Bo Bo!'

He ran towards me and gave me a hug. I broke down and started pleading with him to take me home. My older sister Mary was with him.

'Please, Da. Don't let them take me away. I swear, I'll go to school. I'll never do anything wrong again, please Da, please, please!

'Don't let them take me away, Da. I don't want to leave, I don't want to leave you. Where's Ma?'

Da didn't cry but I knew he was on the verge of tears.

'There's nothing I can do, Bo Bo. Take that. There's sixpence for you.'

He put his arms around me and pulled me close to him. He handed me his lunch.

'I love you, Bo Bo. You are my best boy.'

He held my head and brought me over to his shoulder and hugged me, and told me he loved me. That was the last time my father ever held me and told me that he loved me, although I didn't know it at the time.

The brothers looked at my father sternly, grabbed me by the arm and pulled me onto the train. They were afraid that I would run away. They also turned my head to stop me looking back at my Da. I was hoping he would come over and take me home. I thought he would do something but he didn't. I held that against him for years afterwards but I now know he had no choice.

We got on the train. It was an old train – you could not walk through the carriages. There were small compartments that seated six people with two windows – one on each side. People stared at me because I was bawling crying.

'Don't cry,' said the older of the two brothers. 'You will like it in Upton. There are lots of boys from Dublin there. You will soon get used to it.'

The brothers handed me some sandwiches but I couldn't eat. Da had given me his sandwiches wrapped in paper. I knew that this was his lunch for work.

I started to cry again. I felt a mixture of emotions. I couldn't stop thinking about Ma and Da.

'What's the matter, Maurice?'

'This is me Da's lunch for work and he gave it to me. He won't have anything to eat.'

'He'll be all right. Eat your sandwiches.'

'Do you play football Maurice?'

'Yes. I do.'

'What kind of football do you play?'

'I play soccer.'

'There won't be no soccer. We play Gaelic in Upton and no one is allowed to play soccer.'

The train journey took four hours, which was an eternity to a ten-year-old boy. I had never seen the Irish countryside. When I looked out the window I could see fields, cows, horses and sheep. When we arrived in Cork, another brother met us off the train. He drove us to Upton in a lorry.

I will never forget arriving there. I could see this great big house at the bottom of a long avenue. It looked like a haunted house to me. Then one of the brothers pointed at it and said, 'There's Upton, your new home.'

The lorry turned into a big avenue with a gate lodge on the right-hand side. There were trees on both sides of the avenue and a graveyard on the right-hand side when you passed the gate lodge.

'There is the farm and here is the boiler house,' said one of the brothers.

The truck stopped and we all got out. The brothers brought me into the building through a side door. The place was huge. I followed the brothers into a kitchen, then through a dining hall, out another door and into a prefect's office.

I said to myself, this isn't too bad. The house was bigger than anywhere I'd ever seen. There were boys wandering around everywhere. The brother continued with his guided tour.

'On the right is the wash house. That is where you will wash yourself every morning. The toilets are on the left.'

'Yes, sir.'

I kept nodding at everything he said. But I wasn't listening to a word. Boots' boots were squashing my feet. They were too small for me and my feet were not used to hard leather.

The brother brought me into a room where there were two other brothers waiting. He then left while the others took my clothes off and gave me a school uniform to put on.

There was something about these men which scared me. I felt that I now belonged to them. When I was dressed, they brought me back to the prefect's office and that was where I first met Br. Joe O'Brien.

'Have you any money, Ward?'

I told him I had sixpence and gave it to him. He logged the money into a book but said if I wanted to buy sweets I could. He opened up this press to show me the sweets. He gave me a sweet and looked me straight in the eyes.

'Now you will be a good boy Maurice, won't you?'

'Yes, sir.'

'You will call me Br. O'Brien.'

'Yes, Brother.'

He gave me something to eat and told me to go and play outside. After a few minutes, he brought this young lad over to me. He had red hair.

'This is Thomas. He's from Dublin. He will show you where everything is. Anything you want to know, he will tell you. You will also go with him when it is time for bed.

'He will bring you to the small dorm and show you where your bed is.'

'Okay, Brother.'

'Now, Tommy, bring Maurice around the yard and show him where everything is.'

Tommy was terrified. He wouldn't even look at Br. O'Brien. He never said a word and did exactly what he was told. He showed me where the toilets were, the handball alley, the bookmakers, the tailors, the surgery and even the hall where they showed films once a week.

I cried myself to sleep that night, and for the next few weeks after that. I missed home. I missed Dublin. I would have given anything to go home. But more than anything, I missed Ma and Da. I would have given anything to see them. You never miss your parents until they're gone.

I settled into Upton as best I could. I had no option but to attend school. If I am honest, I would admit that the discipline was good for me. My 'fuck the world' attitude began to disappear. But I could never understand why the boys were so timid and shy. There was no laughter and no one messed in class. The boys were terrified of the brothers. I couldn't exactly say what was wrong but there was a hidden fear among everyone.

I found the answer to that question after six weeks. I was called out of class one morning and told to go to Br. O'Brien's office. I thought he had news from Ma or Da.

I knocked on the door and walked inside.

Br. O'Brien was there with another man I didn't recognise.

'Father, this is Maurice Ward. Maurice this is Fr. Egan.'

Without warning, Fr. Egan turned to me and shouted, 'So you're the boy who gets up early, the boy who gets up before everyone else and steals their clothes.'

'I don't know what you mean.'

'You don't know what I mean?'

'No. I don't know what you mean.'

He came towards me and punched me in the face. The blow knocked me off my feet. It nearly knocked me unconscious.

'Do you know what that means do you?'

Br. O'Brien started laughing at me. The fucking bastard was loving every minute of this.

'Get the strap and give him a few benders. Teach him never to take anything that does not belong to him.'

Fr. Egan grabbed me and started pulling my trousers off. He was like an animal. He grabbed at my arms and legs.

What the fuck was going on? I had been beaten before but there was something different about the way they wanted to punish me. I couldn't describe it. I just knew it was different.

'You bend down and I'll hold your ankles while I teach you a lesson.'

I fought him off as best I could but he got my trousers down. Fr. Egan belted me around the face to keep me still. He then started whipping me. He stood behind me and administered one whip at a time. The pain was unbearable. I screamed in pain but that didn't stop him. Fr. Egan beat me black and blue.

The pain was unbearable. As the tears flowed down my cheeks, the two of them smiled at each other. Now I knew why the boys were afraid.

Br. O'Brien asked me what clothes I had robbed from the house in Glasnevin. I told them everything I had with me.

'What was wrong with your clothes?'

I told them my clothes were torn and my shoes were broken.

'Does that mean you have to steal from other boys?'

Fr. Egan belted me again, this time slapping me across the face. He told me that he was going to send the clothes back to Glasnevin.

'Now get back to class and make sure to stay out of my way.'

chapter four

The leather whip left welts across my backside and back. My ears also swelled up. I couldn't walk properly. The pain from the belt marks was excruciating. Fr. Egan meant to inflict wounds. I knew he hadn't lost his temper and attacked me. I believed he enjoyed it. I believed that he enjoyed beating me, though at the time I couldn't understand why.

I have met members of the Rosminian Order since that day. I know they are good people but I believe some of them in those days were disturbed. There were some brothers who were kind to us but I was afraid of the ones that weren't. The men who abused me have long since died but I still remember the attacks as if they happened yesterday.

I decided there and then that I would run away. At that time, I was palling around with a few kids who lived in the dorm. They were broken boys. The spirit had been beaten out of them. I was determined that I would not end up like them.

I asked one of them did anyone ever run away and they said no. I couldn't understand why they hadn't fled. If you are bold and get slapped, that's no problem. But there was something about the way that some brothers administered punishment that was different. I couldn't stop thinking about it.

I could see the boys were scared. They said the brothers caught everyone who ran away and beat them up. One of the boys even begged me not to do anything stupid.

I will always remember the looks on their faces. I think they were more scared of being implicated in my plan than actually running away. I just couldn't understand them. How could they stay when we were being attacked? I didn't sleep a wink that night. I couldn't stop thinking about the attacks. I had no choice. The welts had blistered and were weeping. Every time I moved I felt excruciating pain but all I could think about was running away. I told a few of the boys that I was going. At the time I thought I could trust them. I planned to go at the weekend. I must admit that I hadn't worked out how I was going to get to Dublin but I didn't care. If I had to live rough and walk the whole way home, I was going.

That same night I was dragged out of my bed and brought downstairs to the office. It was freezing and I only had a long shirt on me.

Br. O'Brien was standing there.

'Are you going to run away, Maurice?'

'No, Br. O'Brien.'

He said nothing and just walloped me on the left temple. I couldn't tell you if he hit me with a stick or not but the whole side of my head and face went numb.

'If you run away I will take this leather and I will beat you black and blue. Do you hear me?'

'Yes, Brother. What have I done?'

He hit me again on the top of my head – this time with a leather strap.

'If you do, you know what will happen, don't you?'

'I won't, Brother. I promise.'

'You'd better not.'

I made my way back to the dormitory. I knew one of the boys had told them I was going to run away. I didn't know who betrayed me. I figured they were scared but that didn't stop me from hating every one of them. I saw them as weak little fucks that had no bottle.

The next morning, Thomas was put in charge of me. He was a nice boy but older and bigger than me. I knew he didn't want the job.

'If you run off, they will kill me. Don't tell them orphans anything. All of them were in one place or another since they were babies. Most of them have no mammies and daddies. They love this place.'

Tommy was trying to be my friend but he was also trying to save his own skin.

I thought he was wrong. No one in their right mind could love Upton but I was wrong. There were lots of kids that loved the school. It took me some time to figure the system out but there were different levels of boys in the school. Some Rosminian brothers hated some boys while others were liked.

Tommy fell somewhere in between. He was someone I could trust because I knew the brothers often beat him. I asked him if anyone had run away.

'Yes, loads of boys do. They bring you back and flog you for days and if you run away they will shave my head and flog me as well.'

Tommy was a nice kid. I didn't know if this was true or not but I was still going. Tommy was very quiet but he let a lot of kids boss him around. That was his way of dealing with Upton. He tried to walk the middle of the road. I suppose he believed he wouldn't get knocked down. I liked Tommy. He had a miserable life. The brothers forced him to work hard in the garden. Although he was given the job of making sure that I wouldn't run away, he became my friend. He would rob an apple or tomato from the garden, tell me to hide it and not to let anyone else see me eat it. I will never forget him for the kindness he showed.

The brothers who beat me didn't show me that sort of kindness. Let me explain what I mean. One day in the handball alley, I was eating an apple that Tommy had nicked. I was still devising my escape plan and my mind was wandering. I didn't notice another brother watching me.

'Where did you get that apple, boy?'

I didn't know what to say to him. When I didn't answer, he told me to go to the office and wait. He took the apple from me and threw it over the wall. I had only started eating it. He was a vicious bastard.

Waiting for him to come to the office was terrifying. When he did eventually arrive, he asked me the same question one more time.

I just stood there and looked at him. I didn't know what to say. There was no way I was going to land Tommy in trouble. He walked over to a press and took out his leather whip.

'Do you hear me?'

He twisted the leather strap in his hand. 'Where did you get the apple?'

'I found it.'

'Where did you find it?'

'At the school steps.'

'Didn't you steal stuff from Marlborough house before you came here?'

'Yes, Brother.'

'You are a little thief, aren't you?'

'Yes, Brother.'

'Where did you get the apple?'

'I found it at the steps of the school,' I said.

'Grab your ankles and then get down.'

He flogged me over and over until my whole body was black and blue and numb all over. He whipped me hard. I cried myself to sleep again but I promised myself I would get out of there no matter what they did to me. I didn't care if they killed me.

I don't know how long I was in Upton when I ran away. I think I was 12-years-old. When you are 12 years of age you think you know it all. I decided to go at night, which would give me a head start.

The brothers employed a man who used to come around at night and wake up the slashers. These were the boys who wet their beds.

He was a cruel man. He would come in, pass our beds and head down to the slashers' wing, which was half way down the dormitory right beside the toilets. He would put his hand beneath the covers and feel the bed.

If the bed was wet, he would beat the boy and send him to the toilet. Then he would put the boy back into the wet bed without changing the bed sheets but that wasn't the end of it.

He would put the boy's name on a list which he gave to the brothers. The brothers would read out all the names the next morning to let everyone know what boys had pissed the bed. If this wasn't enough, they sometimes forced the boys to bring their mattress down and parade all around the yard with the mattress on their backs.

Some of the boys in the school were cruel to the other boys. They would jeer the slashers and call them names. The kids would just cry.

I thought St. Patrick's Industrial School in Upton was hell on earth. Some of the brothers broke our spirits. They designed a regime to denigrate any poor boy sent there.

Watching the boys go through such brutal humiliation re-enforced my commitment to escape. My plan was to run the moment the night porter had finished his rounds. I thought I had prepared well. I had saved up a few pieces of food for my journey. I decided I was going to stay on the railway tracks and the fields but avoid the roads at all costs.

As soon as the night porter finished his tour, I put my clothes in a pillowcase and headed for the toilet. I tossed the covers in my bed. If anyone looked in my bed they would think I was fast asleep in it.

In the toilet, I threw the pillowcase out the window and climbed out. Once I was out and on the ground, I got dressed and headed for the nearest train tracks.

It was about two o'clock in the morning. I remember the night was pitch black and freezing cold with just a little moonlight.

I was terrified. I made my way along the country roads until I reached a train crossing.

I was now on the tracks and on my way to Cork. When the day broke, I decided to go into the fields and stay there for a while. I sat down on a tree stump and thought about my life.

I opened up the lunch that I had and started to eat. The feeling of freedom was great. Although it was freezing cold, I felt elated. I had escaped. I genuinely believed that I would make it home. Sure why wouldn't I?

After I had rested, I began walking again. This time, I headed through the fields but kept close to the tracks. I came across an old farmyard and I went into the hayloft and fell asleep. I woke up later on that evening and went on my way again.

I saw a lot of lights and houses ahead of me, which I avoided should anyone see me.

After what seemed like days of travelling, I found myself on the outskirts of Cork city. I was elated. There was no way they could catch me now.

I was desperate to see normal people again. I headed into a small housing estate and sat there watching life go by. It was great just to see kids and people walking around. I missed my Ma and Da. I remember sitting on a wall and promising myself there and then that I would never get into trouble again.

I found an old shed and decided to sleep there for the night. The next morning, as soon as it got bright, I headed off to find the train station. I walked until I came across two boys my own age and asked them for directions to the train station. They seemed friendly enough and offered to take me there. One of the boys had a bag of bulls-eyes. He handed me a few and I put them in my pocket.

'You go to the top of the road boy and the station is on your right,' he said.

They were sound blokes. On the way to the station, I saw a bread van and couldn't resist the temptation. I went over and looked inside to see if I could find his moneybag.

I don't think he had one because I looked and couldn't find it. But disaster struck when I was looking under the seat. I heard someone shout, 'Hey, what are you doing?'

I looked around to see the breadman coming towards me. I never had any luck with bread vans. I ran off as quick as I could. I went into the train station and asked what time the next train to Dublin left.

The inspector said he didn't know but pointed to a man with a trolley and told me to ask him. The moment I asked the second man I sensed something was wrong. He said he didn't know the timetable but he invited me into his office.

Like a stupid fucking idiot, I followed him inside. He shut the door, grabbed me and pushed me into a smaller office and locked the door.

'What the fuck are you doing?'

'Where's your mother?'

'Up there. I am with my Auntie on holidays.'

'Did you run away from Upton?'

'What's Upton? Where's Upton?'

The game was over. I knew I was dead. I could hear him on the phone talking to someone. I looked for a way out but I couldn't find one. There was no window.

I knew I was fucked. The brothers were about to get me back and there was nothing I could do about it.

A few minutes later I heard a knock. A man opened the door slowly and peered at me.

'You sit down there. You are in big trouble.'

'You will be in big trouble when my Ma finds out what you did to me.'

'We will see, boy.'

He opened the door and another man came in.

'Did you run away from Upton, boy? You'd better tell me the truth.'

'No, I didn't run away from Upton or anywhere else. You wait till me Ma comes down here, you're going to be in big trouble.'

'If anyone is in trouble, you're the boy who's in trouble, not us. Well, the police are on the way, they'll sort it out.'

This was a life or death situation. I knew I had only one chance to escape. As soon as the door opened I dived out and made a run for it.

My heart was pounding. I ran faster than I ever have before or since. I could hear my heart pounding –

thump, thump, thump, thump. I put distance between myself and the CIE workers. They were shouting at people to stop me.

Then this fucking idiot who was about 16 or 17-years-old jumped on me and we hit the ground. I banged my head because he landed on top of me.

'Get the fuck off me. You stupid fucking bastard! You stupid fucking bastard!'

The CIE workers soon had a hold of me. When I scrambled to my feet, there were two gardaí standing there. I was screaming crying, pleading with them to let me go.

The young guy thought he had stopped a bank robbery. He was sticking his chest out and acting like a little hard man holding me down. I had cut my head and was bleeding. The Rosser told him to let me go and handed me a piece of white cloth to stop the bleeding.

'What did you run away for?'

'I didn't run away.'

'What's your name?'

'My name is Johnny Stanley.'

'Turn around son.'

I did as I was told. He tugged at my shirt and looked at the collar. On the inside of my shirt was my name and number. Another Rosser came and took a hold of me.

'We have him,' said the first. 'Beejaysus, you gave us a good run for our money for a small guy like you. Do you know how many people are out looking for you, and the brothers are worried about you.'

A squad car arrived at the station minutes later and they put me in it. I don't know where they brought me but I know it was a Rosser shop.

'Are you hungry, Maurice?'

I said I was starving

'You stay there with him and I'll get him something to eat,' said the older Rosser. 'Don't let him out of your sight.'

And off he went. The Rosser who was left behind asked why I was sent to Upton. I told him for not going to school.

'Do you not like school, Maurice? If you don't go to school, you won't be able to read and write.'

'I don't care.'

'You don't care now, but when you get older you will. Why did you run away from Upton?'

'They are always hitting me. They are whipping me with leather whips.'

I told him about the beatings and the leather. I told him what the brothers were doing to the boys.

'You can tell a good story boy.'

The other Rosser came back with a cup of tea and bread. He asked me if I had ever tasted rhubarb tart. I hadn't.

'Well, Maurice, try some now. You won't get anything like this in Dublin.'

And with that he handed me a bowl of tart with cream. True to his words, I have never tasted anything like it. It was beautiful.

He brought me out to another room and the first person I saw was Br. Joe O'Brien. He looked all concerned but I knew he was going to torture me when he got me alone.

The brother thanked the gardaí for finding me and promised to talk some sense to me. He took me by the arm and escorted me to a car parked outside.

He never said a word on the way back to Upton. He just boxed me in the thigh. As we drove in the avenue, he told me I would not run away again. He brought me through the kitchen and the dining hall where all the boys were having their tea. They were all looking at me. They knew what was about to happen.

As we left the dining hall I turned left to go to the prefect's office but Br. O'Brien said, 'This way.'

He brought me towards Fr. Spellman's office. On our way there we met one of the brothers.

'Well, how is our little runaway? Do you know the trouble you have caused for so many people?'

He punched me on the side of the head. I started to bleed down the left side of my face.

'Take him down there and then bring him to the prefect's office.'

Br. O'Brien brought me into Fr. Spellman's office. He was a little fat man who wore thick glasses. When he saw the blood trickling down my face, he asked what had happened.

'One of the brothers did it to me.'

Br. O'Brien grabbed me by the back of the neck and called me a liar.

'That happened down in Cork when a boy jumped on him and tried to catch him for the gardaí.'

I then got another few slaps.

'Maurice, we can't put up with this; boys running away. Why did you run away?' Fr. Spellman asked.

I told him I missed me Ma and Da.

'Well, your Ma and Da can't help you now.'

He got up and came to me. He lifted his right hand but slapped me on the left hand side of my face. The blood trickled down my face again.

'Get him out of here before I kill him.'

This was the green light for Br. O'Brien to beat me. He grabbed me by the front of the jumper, drew me right up to his face and told me, 'If you ever run away again, I promise you, you will regret it.'

'Get him out of here!' roared Fr. Spellman. Br. O'Brien turned me to the door and gave me a kick in the back which sent me flying into the hallway. He followed me out, grabbed me by the neck and dragged me to the prefect's office.

One of the brothers was already sitting there grinning when I arrived. They all seemed to have the same evil grin.

'Take off your shoes and stockings.'

I did as instructed.

'Take off your jumper and shirt.'

I did.

'Now take off your trousers.'

I did. They brought me into the wash house where they beat the shit out of me. I was in bed for days after the beating. They had different boys stay with me on and off for a few weeks after I'd run away.

One of the boys they put in charge of me was a big fucker. He told me he would kill me if I ran away.

'You run away again and I will kill you. The brothers won't have to. I will kill you myself. If you run away again, I will kill you.

'Come back and I will kick you all around the place. Do you hear me?'

He then started hitting me.

'Do you hear me? You fucking Dublin bastard.'

Thankfully Tommy was put in charge of me when I was allowed out to play again. I was glad. I knew he would not hit me.

'It's no use running away, Maurice. They will kill you. Believe me, they will kill you.'

'Fuck them.'

'Maurice, don't run away when I'm minding you.'

'I won't, Tommy, I won't get you into trouble.'

They put me in the room off the small dorm where I slept on my own. The room was right beside the prefect's bedroom. They punished me for months afterwards. I was not allowed to go to the pictures or eat sweets.

I didn't care. I could take the beatings. The more they gave me, the stronger I grew. But things were about to take a turn for the worse.

chapter five

Things eventually returned to normal, if there was such a thing as normality inside the walls of St. Patrick's Industrial School in Upton. I tried to avoid trouble. I suppose I had come to terms with my situation. I missed Ma and Da but I came to accept that I wasn't going home soon. Looking back now, I think some of the Rosminian brothers realised my change in attitude because they didn't pay much attention to me. They let me get on with my life as best I could. They moved me back into the dormitory with the other boys. I interpreted the move as a good sign and I even started paying attention in class. When they gave me a job in the pantry I was ecstatic but it would prove the beginning of my worst nightmare. It was here that I was first sexually abused.

I still find it difficult to talk about what happened back then. I denied it to myself for years. I never spoke about it to anyone. The sexual abuse turned me into a man who resorted to extreme violence. I am now homophobic and hate the Catholic Church with a vengeance. I have nightmares. I wake at night screaming for help. I can remember the abuse as if it happened yesterday. I know it will haunt me until the day I die. When I was a boy I didn't know what the word paedophile meant. I do now.

The first person to sexually abuse me was Br. Buglar. He was in charge of the pantry. All the boys at Upton knew him because we were told he invented the school's Black Pudding Stew. He was different from the other brothers. He didn't beat the boys with the same ferocity as some of the others but he did torture them in his own perverted way.

When I think about him I feel like murdering someone. He started abusing me when I started working in the pantry.

I noticed Br. Buglar looking at me. He wasn't looking at what I was doing. He just had this look in his eye. I couldn't make him out. He was looking at me rather than at what I was doing. I took no notice of him.

I continued with my chores. Every so often I would glance at Br. Buglar through the corner of my eye. He would glance back. This went on for ages. Br. Buglar then called me into a small room where dried peas, herbs and that sort of thing were stored. He kept making eye contact, which struck me as unusual.

'Will you get me the blue tin on the top shelf?'

'Will I climb up and get it?'

'Yes, Maurice. Climb up there.'

I knew he was up to something. I half expected him to accuse me of robbing some food and start beating me. But when I began to climb, Br. Buglar put his arms on my backside, almost as if he was trying to balance me. I didn't see anything wrong with this so I took no notice of him. I just thought he was a bit strange.

I grabbed the tin and started to make my way back down. But Br. Buglar didn't let go. He held me there squeezing my bottom. I thought he was doing this by accident but then he put his right hand inside my shirt and started rubbing my chest. I remember thinking, 'What the fuck's going on here?'

Then he put his left hand up the leg of my trousers. I froze. I didn't know what to do. He kept moving his hand until he grabbed my privates. When I say I froze, I mean I actually froze solid. The blood drained from my face and I began to shake.

I think this turned him on. He pulled me closer until I could feel his breath on the back of my neck. I couldn't move. I wanted to hit him or try beat him off but I couldn't move. I felt like getting sick but I couldn't. I stood there like a fucking fool with him kissing the back of my neck and groping me.

He kissed and bit the back of my neck. I remember feeling the stubble of his chin rubbing against my neck. It was disgusting. It seemed to go on forever.

He played with my privates and then my backside. He would stroke my thighs then cup my privates into his hand. The more aroused he became, the more he kissed me.

I would later learn that abusers are all the same. They get a kick out of forcing children to perform masturbation on them.

Br. Buglar was no different. He took my hand in his and placed it on his private parts. He made me rub him up and down, up and down. I didn't know what I was doing or even what to do. I was so afraid. My hand shook with fear but this only turned him on even more. I didn't say anything. I don't know how long it lasted, but it seemed to last forever. Time stood still.

The attack was the first of many although it's the one I most vividly recall.

I don't think Br. Buglar would remember what I even looked like if he was still alive. But I can remember everything about him. He was a revolting looking bastard of the highest order.

He dressed differently from the rest. Even before he abused me, I was scared of him. In fact, all the boys were scared of him. We thought he looked like Dracula.

Br. Buglar was very tall and very dark. He brushed his hair straight back and wore a long, black cloak. He thought he looked religious but the boys thought he looked like a monster from a horror film. When he walked through the corridors, the cloak trailed behind him.

The sex abuse was a power thing with him. Part of him liked controlling me. Another part of him was a pervert. It was a power play thing with him. I find this hard to say but he got his kick out of examining young boys' private parts.

Br. Buglar destroyed my life. He took away what was left of my childhood. He attacked me about three times a week. There was no way of escaping.

I don't need to tell you that I had nowhere to turn. Can you imagine what they would have done to me if I went to one of the brothers and said what was happening? I believe that some of the kinder brothers would have done something but I was too afraid. I closed down. I lost my self-respect. I quickly became aware that other boys were being interfered with but none of us spoke about it. I certainly didn't understand what Br. Buglar was doing to me. I just knew it was wrong.

The abuse wasn't confined to the pantry. He would follow me around and ask me into a private room. He even abused me on the farm. The bastard used to follow me into the barn and ask me to get something in the loft. I knew what would inevitably happen. He would follow me up to the loft and grab me from behind. The abuse had by this time gotten worse. He'd hold me close and force my hand inside his cossack. It was disgusting. He would turn me around and start kissing me on the face. I know it sounds mad but he looked on boys like me as being dirty. When he forced me to feel him, he would always force me to touch him outside his pants so I didn't feel his bare flesh. I think he managed to convince himself in his own twisted mind that I was somehow responsible and his crimes were more justified once I didn't actually feel his skin.

He was mad. He was evil. He loved abusing me. I came to recognise that look I mentioned earlier. I always knew when he was going to interfere with me.

At night he would come into the dormitory and do the same thing. It was always the same. He used to come up and sit on my bed. He would always make sure to pull back his cloak, which covered most of the bed. That would stop the other boys from seeing what was going on; not that they needed anyone to tell them.

There was no escaping him. He would sit on the left hand side of my bed. He would then pretend to read a book holding it with his right hand. He would then put his left hand under the bedclothes and touch me. He would stroke me and do things that I have spent my whole life trying to forget. He would do what he liked, then head off before we said our prayers. I believe the bastard abused me and then prayed for forgiveness. He was a sick pervert and I hope he is rotting in hell.

But Br. Buglar wasn't the only paedophile who worked with the boys in Upton. The brothers employed a local handyman called Davy Ormond who used to help himself to the boys' bodies. Ormond was a giant of a man. He lived in a small cottage near Upton Railway Station, near the Post Office if I remember right.

I was in the kindling room one day and he grabbed me. He held me close and just put his hand down my trousers and began feeling me. I pulled away and told him that I was having none of it. He stopped and never tried it again.

But he got his own back on me. The boys used to line up once a week in front of him. He would examine our stockings for holes. If he didn't like you, he would make a hole in the stocking with his fingers, then beat the shit out of you.

He used to beat everyone up. He did the same thing to everyone. He would catch you by the hair on the temple above your ear and lift you off the ground. When he beat me up, he boxed me in the face and kicked me at the same time. Other times he would just stamp on my toes. While he was doing this, he would shout, 'I think you need some more elbow grease boy.'

Upton, for some reason, attracted some violent and disturbed men back in those days. I remember one of the teachers that I had, who is long since dead, used to masturbate at the back of the class. He would order us to stare at the blackboard while he masturbated. It became the biggest joke among the boys.

He made us look straight ahead while he played pocket billiards. That's what we called it. Pocket Billiards. If we looked around to see what he was doing, he would beat us up with the leg of an old chair.

We never learned anything in his class because he was more interested in being a pervert than teaching us.

The boys were never taught about sex or the facts of life. I certainly didn't know anything about homosexuality. I learned about sex by watching a pig giving birth, but even that lesson was mired by extreme violence that left me injured.

Punishment was a part of everyday life in Upton. Boys from my background could expect to be slapped a few times each day but we were often beaten severely which left us physically and mentally scared. I remember those beatings with clarity.

Fr. Egan was one of the most violent people I have ever met. I haven't met many gangsters that would have the same propensity for violence as he did. He was the most vicious of them all.

One attack happened when I was working on the farm. Fr. Egan was the man in charge of the farm. He was a vicious bastard but if you did your work and did it well, he would leave you alone. You might think I'm mad when I say this but he would actually be nice to you. He had this way about him. He would say, 'Come on boys, let's get to work.'

He could be great. No, I stand corrected. He could be better than great to boys who had no family. The work in the fields was fulfilling. You learned new things every day.

I grew to love working on the farm because I was near animals. There were no farm animals in Dublin, even back then. It was great.

I had everything down to a tee and I was doing good work. I genuinely loved the work.

While Fr. Egan was unpredictable, I had slowly come to trust him. One day he introduced me to this big boy who worked on the farm. He was much older than me, he was about 18-years-old. I think he was in the school himself and when he turned 16 they gave him a job on the farm. Anyway, his name was Hank.

One day, Fr. Egan told Hank to watch a sow that was about to give birth to her piglets. This was great. I loved the fact that he trusted me enough to work with Hank.

Fr. Egan led me into a shed where I saw the pig caged in an iron crate. She was lying on her side with a bar holding her down.

Fr. Egan told me the bar would stop the pig rolling over on the little banbhs when they were born. I didn't know how anything was born. I think Fr. Egan knew by the way that I looked at him that I hadn't a clue what was about to happen.

'Did you ever see anything being born, Maurice?

'No, Father. I never did.

'Well, Hank will show you everything you need to know.'

Hank was a great fella. He explained everything to me. I learned more in those few seconds from him than I did from anybody else in Upton during my time there. Hank showed me where the little piglets came out and exactly what to expect when the piglets were born. He said the sow would lick the banbhs but I was to move them to one side when she was finished.

To say I was really excited is an understatement. I had never seen anything being born. But the fact that Fr. Egan now trusted me with such an important job meant more to me. The last time I felt that particular emotion was after the cake shop job in the old tenement.

Hank left me with the sow while he had a cup of tea. He told me not to worry because Mother Nature would look after the banbhs. Nothing happened for an hour so I went off to the toilet but when I came back I found three little piglets. They were just the best things ever. I wanted to cuddle them but I did what I was told. I picked them up and put them beside the sow where they could suckle just like Hank showed me.

The three little pigs seemed fine to me. It was then that I noticed a chord sticking out of their bellies. I didn't know what it was but I started to pull the chord from one of them. I also tried to pull the chord from the other two, but my hand kept slipping from it.

Hank appeared just in time and told me to leave it alone.

'Don't ever do that – you will kill them.'

I said I was sorry. Hank said it was fine and explained what an umbilical chord was. I was amazed. The sow gave birth to the rest of the banbhs. There were lots of them. I think there was about ten altogether.

When she finished giving birth, Hank went off and came back with Fr. Egan. He took off his jacket, rolled his shirtsleeves up and began looking at the piglets one by one. But three of them were dead.

He asked Hank what happened. I said nothing so Hank told him I had pulled at the chord but he wasn't sure if the banbhs were the ones I had touched. But Hank didn't need to say any more.

Fr. Egan turned around and punched me in the face. The blow sent me flying. I landed a few feet away only to see him grab a pitchfork. He raised it up and belted me. I covered my head with my arms. He kept screaming at me.

'You bastard! I'll show you. You bastard! You little bastard!'

I got away from him at one stage but he caught me again. He beat me black and blue.

I screamed for help and I pleaded with him to stop. It was no use but I kept pleading with him.

I don't know what happened but I woke up on the ground with Hank beside me. Fr. Egan was back looking at the dead piglets.

'Get him out of here, before I kill him.'

Hank said nothing. I couldn't walk properly. There was something wrong with my left leg and my hand. I couldn't put my leg on the ground because it was too painful. The pain in my arm was excruciating.

Hank helped me to the dormitory and I got into bed. There were lumps all over me.

When I woke the next day, my ankle and legs were swollen and I had to limp to walk. On my way down the stairs, a man called Fr. Dalton asked what was wrong with me.

I told him that my leg was swollen. He gave me a slap across the face and told me I deserved it for killing the piglets.

chapter six

In the face of the beatings, mental torture and sex abuse, the boys at St. Patrick's Industrial School in Upton survived. We relied on each other for support. We became best friends to each other because there was no one else we could turn to for help. We believed that no one would ever understand the brutality we suffered.

Some of the brothers were good men but others were animals. The sad thing is that I can only remember the bad ones.

My best friend was Seanie Morrisey from Greenmount in Cork city. We just bonded together and became inseparable. I would die for Seanie. We were never too far from one another. He was a good fella.

Not alone did I grow close to him, I became close to his family. Although I went home for the summer holidays, Ma and Da couldn't afford to come visit me in Upton for the rest of the year. The only bit of motherly love I got during my early teenage years was from Seanie's mother and his sister Eileen. They used to dote on me when they came down to visit Seanie at the weekends. Mrs. Morrisey was a lovely lady.

I used to wonder what would have happened if I hadn't become friends with Seanie. Would I have gone insane or committed suicide over the abuse? I believe the kindness of his family saved me.

You might recall that I mentioned the infliction of mental abuse on the boys. Some of the brothers subjected us to extreme forms of mental abuse. Some of them committed the most depraved acts. I will never understand what caused these brothers to be so bitter. One particular brother used to force the boys to work as slaves for him and if we didn't perform to expectations, he would beat us.

He liked to force me to do his bidding. When I say his bidding, I don't mean have sex with him or anything like that. He would force me to act like a slave. Here's what I mean.

He saw himself as an all-round sportsman. He played golf and considered himself a gunman. Every week, he would pick two or three boys and take us out to a field. We would carry his golf clubs while he walked ahead. When he found a suitable place, he would take a golf ball out of his pocket, push a tee into the ground and place a ball down. He would then ask me to hand him a driver, and he would hit the ball as far as he could.

Anyone could see he was a crap golfer but he could hit the ball. I still don't know whether he did this on purpose or by accident but he'd usually whack the ball into a clump of trees or nettles.

With that he'd tell us to fetch the ball. He treated us like dogs.

I still have problems talking about this. Was he a cruel bastard or sick in his head? I don't know but I can tell you that he tortured me. If I didn't find the ball, he would leave me there until I found it. He treated me like a retriever; like a fucking dog.

While this was his attempt at mental torture, it failed. I used to steal golf balls from his office. When he called me to play the part of his Labrador, I always made sure that I had two golf balls in my pocket. I would produce these when I couldn't find the balls he had walloped off into the distance.

He thought he was a smart bastard but I was smarter. I would bring the golf balls back no matter where he hit them, much to his frustration. I soon got the upper hand.

He did the same kind of thing when he went out shooting pheasants. The fucking bastard actually had dogs but he wouldn't let the dogs do the running around. I don't think the dogs were trained. It didn't matter because he made us do it.

Helping this brother to hunt was worse than collecting golf balls. We were young boys. He forced us to pick up poor little birds he had shot. The birds would have their chests shot open and their wings broken.

Sometimes I found birds that were still alive. I would pick them up and bring them to him. He wouldn't be long killing them. He would choke them by twisting their necks.

Cruelty was part and parcel of life inside Upton if you were not liked. Some of the brothers would abuse you physically and sexually for most of the year then give you a bottle of lemonade at Easter and Christmas. They made this nonsense out to be a big deal. Some of the good brothers would come out with bowls of eggs at Easter and hand them out while preaching the word of the Lord. I knew that the good men could never understand why we were afraid of them. What more can I say?

You may be wondering what happened to my family. Life went on for Ma and Da. They had more children while I was locked away. I used to visit the family in Dublin every summer but I'd be lying if I said that we didn't grow apart. Ma and Da never wrote to me. They couldn't read or write. I was still a member of the family but I was a distant one. I was someone that was there but I wasn't really there, if you know what I mean.

Some of the brothers bullied me over this. When the mail would come for the other boys, I would go along with my pals to collect their post.

I didn't need anyone to tell me there were no letters there for me. I will always remember standing with my friends and one would get a letter and shout, 'I got five shillings; Ma and Da sent down five shillings.'

The money would be in a postal order. I thought it was great. I was happy for them. I wouldn't get jealous or anything. We would all read the letters. We would give each other moral support.

I will always remember standing there and Br. Dalton or Br. O'Brien coming over and asking me what I was doing.

Br. O'Brien used to make a point of shouting out loud, 'Everyone knows that you don't get letters.'

I'd just nod my head and move away. I knew this already but I didn't need to be reminded. He would say it in front of everybody to let them know; the funny thing was that everyone already knew. If Br. O'Brien had any intelligence, he wouldn't have said silly things like that. Those two brothers were more childish than the boys themselves.

I often think back and ask were they just insane. What sort of person would act like that? Those two seemed to enjoy inflicting mental torture on the boys.

Although I hated everything about Upton I also experienced some acts of humanity there. I was lucky enough to befriend a man called Mya Lynch. He was a famous footballer who visited the boys. He used to give his spare time to the boys in Upton. He lived in Cork city but he was kind enough to drive down to Upton on Friday nights and stay 'till Sunday mornings.

Mya was our hero. Sometimes he would take a couple of the boys off on day trips. He would bring them into Cork city, give them money and let them go shopping.

He was a kind man. There was nothing in it for him. He was just trying to be a good Christian.

One Christmas he brought me to visit a family in Cork called the O'Mahonys. Mya told them that I was a good little fella who never got into trouble. No one had ever said that about me before. I could have cried. He was genuinely proud to know me. He was proud of all the boys. We thought he was the greatest person to walk the face of the earth.

As you would expect, the O'Mahony family were decent people. I don't think Mya would have known anyone who wasn't genuine. He was that sort of fella.

The family treated me like one of their own and started taking me away for weekends. Sometimes they would come down and see me. They were lovely people, they looked after me and they treated me as if I was one of their own. The family didn't have much money themselves but what they did have, they were willing to share.

I grew very close to Mr. and Mrs. O'Mahony. I remember telling them about the violence in Upton but they didn't say much. They didn't call me a liar or anything; I think they just didn't know whether to believe me or what to do. I didn't mention it again in case I frightened them away.

I always hated going back to the school after spending time with them. I used to cry and sink into a depression. I would be so afraid. There were some good brothers but I was afraid to talk. The whole thing was terribly frightening for a young boy. It was dreadful.

Life inside the walls of Upton never changed. Life was the same day in and day out. We'd be woken in the morning to say our prayers. We attended Mass everyday before breakfast. If you had any chores, you did them as soon as breakfast was over. In the mornings, I worked in Fr. McVadden's office. He was a good man. In fact, he was very kind to me. I used to light his fire and dust around the office. Other boys had other jobs in the houses where the brothers lived.

Some boys made their beds and cleaned their rooms. I always thought the boys ran the whole school under the supervision of superiors. The boys brushed the floors, cleaned the windows – anything that had to be done – the boys did the work.

When you were finished the chores, you went to school. When I think back on it – I was sent down there for not going to school, but yet when I got there, I didn't learn much. I didn't have a chance. I would have learned more on the streets.

Dinner was served after noon. After we ate our meals, the boys were allowed into the yard to play. The whistle used to blow at 1.30 p.m. sending us back into class until 2.30 p.m.

Everybody went back to work for the evening; there were no exceptions. Tea was served around 4.00 p.m. That was usually the last thing I got to eat for the day. I got nothing else after that.

I will always remember being hungry down there. I'll never forget the hunger. Hunger drove the boys to rob orchards and steal from the pantry and greenhouses. I scavenged for food. If I was out in the fields retrieving like a fucking Labrador, I would dig up a few raw carrots or sugar beet and eat them.

This may seem innocent enough but it was a highly dangerous thing to do. If one of the vicious brothers saw you eating outside of meal times they would punish you. I always threw the vegetables I stole in the fields into the ditch so no one would see that I had eaten more than dinner. I couldn't take the risk.

I would eat any edible berries on the trees. I don't believe I got sufficient food to keep me going because I was always hungry. No matter what I ate I was always hungry.

Looking back on those days, I believe hunger forced the boys to bully each other. Each table in the dining room seated six to eight people and a head guy. When the potatoes would come out in a big bowl, the big guy would take his choice of food, whoever was second in charge would take his, by the time it would come to the last guy, there could be nothing left but maybe two little marble-like potatoes. No one cared about the younger guys.

The bigger boys pushed the smaller boys around and would take their food. The smaller boys sometimes got nothing. This happened to me when I went down there first. When I got the run of the place myself, I let nobody push me around. I just decided there was no way anybody was going to hit me again and that was the end of it. When I started to develop a little and grew more confident I began to fight back against the system. I actually threatened to murder one of the brothers after he attacked me. I was released from Upton not long after. This is what happened.

I was woken one night by the sound of a boy screaming. Br. Dalton was beating a friend of mine called George. I could hear George screaming for mercy but Br. Dalton was having none of it. He kept punching and kicking the boy. The bastard was dragging George along the ground while kicking him at every opportunity. George was a slim boy yet Br.

Dalton would not stop kicking and punching him. I listened to George's screams for as long as I could bear before I did something that was unexpected to me. In a moment of pure anger, I jumped out of bed and told Br. Dalton to leave George alone.

I was 15-years-old. I felt a rush of adrenaline flowing through my veins. Br. Dalton looked at me in complete shock not knowing what to say or how to react. At that moment, the entire dormitory woke up and began staring at Br. Dalton. I believe he felt intimidated.

For that moment, the future consequences of my actions did not matter. I had suffered five years of abuse. Now I was fighting back.

Still looking at me in disbelief, Br. Dalton walked over to my bed, grabbed me by the hair and dragged me into his room. I resisted him which made him slightly nervous.

'Get your hands off me.'

He looked shocked. A few of the boys giggled at him, which sent him into a nervous rage. He pushed me out of the bed. I remember walking into the room ahead of him because he punched me in the back of the head.

He slammed the door shut and belted the living daylights out of me. He forced me to the ground where he punched me in the jaw and kicked me in the teeth. He stood on top of me, then pulled an old cabinet dresser down on me. It fell on my legs. When he finished punching me, he dragged me back to bed making sure every one of the boys saw what had happened to me.

There was blood everywhere. He had knocked a few of my teeth out and my jaw was swollen. I was lucky. If the cabinet had hit me on the head, I would have died.

When I woke the next morning, I couldn't walk. Br. Dalton knew he had gone too far. I think he was afraid to take me to a doctor. So I was left to my own devices. A young boy called Tommy looked after me.

Tommy put me in a boxcar we used to move turf and wheeled me around. I don't know where Tommy is now but if you are reading this I'd like to say thanks. I never forgot your kindness.

The attack drove me insane. I felt like murdering Br. Dalton. I saw him and the rest of my abusers as bastards. The only thing that prevented me from murdering him was my age. But as I received more beatings I felt an inner anger develop.

Weeks after that attack, Br. Joe O'Brien came at me in the handball alley while I was playing. I hit him in the face by accident with the ball. He was smoking a cigarette at the time and when the ball hit him sparks flew from the cigarette. I'm sure he must have burnt his lips because he went nuts. He grabbed me and dragged me across the yard by my jumper. My jumper came off in his hands.

He lost control and started screaming out loud. He was like a deranged animal. He punched the living daylights out of me.

That night I started to have fantasies about torturing my abusers. The more beatings I received, the more I started to plan what I was going to do.

The final straw came when myself and George were caught stealing an apple and a tomato in the greenhouse.

Br. Joe O'Brien and Br. Dalton caught us and brought us to the wash house. They attacked the two of us with relish. The beating was so bad, they had to bring us to a hospital. I don't know if it was a hospital or not but there was a nurse and a doctor there.

Br. Dalton spoke to the doctor after warning us to keep our mouths shut. I wanted to tell them what happened but we couldn't say anything because the two brothers were with us all the time. I bit my tongue.

It was clear to anyone with eyes in their head that I was being treated like a dog and beaten like a dog. I had had enough. I told myself that I was strong. Having been beaten more times than I dared admit, I decided now was the time to act.

Grown men were beating me and I was only a boy. So I decided no one was going to hit me again. I made up a knife from a piece of leadpipe and I waited for Br. Dalton in the yard one night.

I will never forget what happened. He was walking along minding his own business when I stepped out of the shadows. He turned as white as a ghost. I approached him and put the knife to him.

'I don't care if I go to prison or if the others fucking kill me. They can do whatever they want to do to me. But if you ever put your fucking hand on me again, I mean it, I'll slit your fucking throat when you're in bed.

'I'll stab you to death. You are nothing but a fucking bastard. You touch me or my friends again and I will fucking murder you in your bed and I'll tell the Rossers what's going on in here.'

He looked at me with big frightened eyes. I saw a different man to the bastard that I knew. He was scared. This guy was afraid. I knew I had this bastard where I wanted him.

'Do you fucking understand what I am saying?'

He nodded his head. I was prepared to murder him that night. I expected him to take revenge but he never did.

I was discharged from Upton on the 31 January 1962 after my Da wrote a letter to the Minister for Education pleading with him to release me. I have a copy of the letter. I had been due for release in March but the letter worked.

The only possessions I had when I left Upton were a drab suit they gave me, and a warrant allowing me to travel to Dublin. I emerged penniless.

Upton was a hell hole. Leaving there was both the best and worst day of my life. I lost my friends, which I found unbearable. I was filled with mixed emotions. It is an understatement to say I emerged from the industrial system a disturbed and violent youngster.

Before I was sent to Upton, I was a mischievous young fella. I had robbed and thieved and did a lot of bad things. But I did what every other kid from my community did.

St. Patrick's Industrial School in Upton changed me. It made me into the kind of boy who rebelled against authority.

In later years I often wondered, even after I got out of there, if they ever thought about what they were doing to us.

When we were young boys, sometimes we would ask if they were really the servants of God. I used to say that if the men who beat me were, there was no way I was going to believe in God or his servants either.

I now feel bitter towards religion. I feel very bitter towards anybody who introduces himself as a man of the cloth; be they a priest, a bishop or a brother. I don't trust them; I could never trust them. I don't believe anyone who speaks for the Church. I have met members of the Rosminian order. They have said sorry. I know they are genuinely sorry for what happened. I believe the people in charge of the Rosminian Order now are good men who are true to their word. They are horrified about what happened and hurt. I know the Rosminians are good men but I am also hurt.

Maybe some day I will come to terms with my past and not tar all the clergy with the same brush. I know what you are thinking. It is okay for you to say you can't blame them all for what happened. But that's easy for you to say. I have no doubt that some of the brothers back then didn't know about the sexual abuse but they knew we were being beaten. They should have done something to stop the violence.

I left Upton with an attitude. I wanted to cause havoc. It was payback time for the society that sent me there.

chapter seven

The sexual and physical abuse I suffered at the hands of the clergy stayed with me for the rest of my life. The regime left me mentally and physically scarred, although I didn't realise it at the time. I used to think Upton drove me to a life of crime. It didn't, but it did transform me into someone capable of extreme violence.

I came to hate everything about religion and the Church; I hated authority most of all but the tragedy was that I came to hate myself more. I grew to hate everything about myself and I despised everyone else.

I dreamed about the sexual abuse most nights. I would wake up in a cold sweat. I used to dream about Br. Buglar touching me, his fucking dirty hands groping me and forcing me to pull him off.

I used to ask myself why I hadn't murdered him. I screamed out loud at night. I would ask myself why I didn't get a knife, creep into his room in the middle of the night and slit his fucking throat. I fantasised about him drowning in his own blood. I used to imagine what he would look like; lying there with his throat slashed, spitting out blood. I wanted to kill the bastard.

I don't know how many times I asked myself that same question. Why didn't I kill him? If I was honest, I would say that I came to blame myself for everything that happened. If I didn't kill him then I must have liked it; this was my logic. I was mad. I was screwed-up.

Did I give him the wrong impression? Did he think I was a queer and I actually liked him?

You might also ask about my relationship with Ma and Da. You are probably wondering what happened. The answer is simple; I had grown apart from them. I moved back home because I had nowhere else to live. Life for my family had moved on. I can't really say any more than that because I don't fully understand what happened myself.

When I was sent to Upton, I suppose I buried my fears. The moment they freed me, all that anger came spilling out. I know all of this now because I've been counselled and I understand my life. But back then I knew nothing. The only thing I knew for sure was that

I could trust no one and I wanted to get even. I hated everyone.

Sexual abuse of the kind I suffered makes you immune to pain. It also fucks you up. I came out of Upton wanting to prove to myself that I wasn't a queer. This is why I ran wild with women. I also returned to the crime scene not giving two fucks if I was caught. If you got in my way, I'd cut your throat. I'm telling you this now to let you know where I was coming from.

My family had moved into a new flat on Sheriff Street in the north inner city. The new address suited me down to the ground. Sheriff Street was the meanest working-class area in Dublin. There were no jobs for young guys like me. The only way I could turn a few quid was through thieving.

I didn't join a gang or anything. In those days, the boys used to meet up to do a bit of work. At the time I worked with this guy called John Gilligan. I was 16-years-old and he was a master thief. You could say he was my mentor.

Old Gilligan used to take me around to the shops in north Dublin and we'd clean them out when the shops closed for lunch. He was a small little fella with a dark complexion. He robbed to get money for the boozer and betting.

Even though he spent most of his life on the piss, he was a great robber. When I say great, I mean the fella was a genius. He had loads of tricks. The one I remember most was a trick he used to open locked doors.

Gilligan used to force doors open by walloping them with his backside. I never knew how he did it but it worked. He was the weirdest little fucker. He had this way about him. He would slam his backside against a door and it would just pop open.

In we'd go and fleece the place, taking everything we could carry; Gillette razor blades, sweets, sugar and all the money from the till. Gilligan always took the lion's share.

I spent my money on women. You might recall that I said I wanted to prove to the world I was not a queer. My way of proving this was to sleep with every girl that I could. I fucked all around me.

In those days, the boys and girls all just hung around together. No one asked anyone out. You just bonded with girls.

My first girlfriend was *Kathleen.* She was the first girl I was with in a sexual way.

We were all going to the picture house and the different couples sat in different places. I don't remember what film was showing because I had no interest in it. I don't mind telling you I was there for one thing alone.

I was giving her some of my sweets and she was giving me some of hers. I'd say we were about 16-years-old. Well, one thing led to another and I was putting my hand over and feeling her leg, and not only feeling her leg, and she had her hand on me and she wasn't just feeling my leg. We ended up leaving the pictures and going down an alley at the back of the North Strand. That was the first sexual experience I ever had with a girl.

I was like a dog chasing a bitch in heat, sitting outside her door waiting for her to come out; I was getting her any way I could. I wanted to prove to everyone that I was no queer.

I was insatiable. I didn't want a relationship. I wanted to screw as many women as possible to prove a point. I became obsessed with having women. I was a slut. I didn't care what they looked like as long as they would do what I wanted.

Money and women became my sole aim in life. I got little jobs here and there. I worked as a messenger boy for a butcher's shop on Parnell Street. I think I used to get seven and six or five shillings a week, I'm not sure now. I used to give Ma half a crown and I'd keep a half-crown myself.

I tried my hand at everything but crime was the only way to make serious money. I'd ask everyone I met for advice on how to get a good job. But I'd always start thieving again. You name the scam, I did it.

I remember I met one or two young guys in Sheriff Street who used to sell papers to sailors on the ships docked in Dublin Port. At that time the docks was a bristling place with ships from all foreign countries.

We'd talk our way on to the ships by pretending we were selling papers.

Once the captain would have his back turned, we'd clean the place out and rob the cabins. I stole everything – cigarettes, watches, lighters and money. I never felt guilty. I didn't give a fuck about the sailors.

Once I'd have a few quid, I'd be off buying a nice bit of clobber to try to make myself as good as everybody else. If you wore the right clobber and were willing to spend a few quid, the women would do anything. And I mean anything.

I was out of Upton about four months when I ended up in trouble with the law. Only this time I was actually innocent. I was in the flats having a chat with a friend of mine who lived close by. We were in the middle of a conversation when he saw the police up at my door.

'Look Bo Bo! The Rossers are up with your Da.'

I looked up and saw Da out on the balcony having a chat with the filth.

'What the fuck do they want? There must be trouble.'

One of the gardaí walked into our house so I ran upstairs to see what was going on. When I walked in the door, Da turned around and said, 'That's him there.' I didn't know what the fuck he was talking about. The Rosser turned around and pointed at my little sister's bike.

'Do you own this bike?'

Da was standing behind the Rosser nodding at me.

'Tell him you own the bike, son.'

I nodded and said nothing. I was trying to work out exactly what was going on.

'Where did you get it?'

'I found it.'

'Where did you find it.'

'At the back of the Church.'

'Okay. I am going to charge you with robbing the bike.'

'But I didn't rob the bike.'

'Doesn't matter. Why didn't you bring it to the gardaí? I'm charging you with stealing by finding.'

'Is this a joke?'

'No. Get your jacket. You are coming with me.'

Da said nothing. He just stood there and stared at the ground. The garda brought me up to Store Street Garda Station and charged me. I was only a few months out of Upton. I ended up getting nine months in St. Patrick's Institution on the North Circular Road for something I didn't do.

Da had bought the bike for my little sister Brigid. The gardaí had seen Brigid cycling the bike around the flats. I think they knew it was stolen. I know Da was trying to protect Brigid but he threw me to the wolves.

I was put into prison for nine months for something I didn't do. Just like in Upton, I got six years for something I never did – that was not going to fucking school.

St. Patrick's was a Borstal. The place was full of boys that came from the industrial school system. There were also hard men; guys that had been in jail most of their lives. They were the true Borstal boys. I met prisoners inside St. Patrick's that boxed and trained hard all day long. These guys kept themselves fit, lean and ready for action. I always thought they were unique among the criminal population.

I know this might sound crazy but I believe Borstal was good for me. I started boxing; I even won a few fights. The moment you start boxing everyone stops fucking you around. I still don't know if it's the muscle or whether your personality changes.

I became the cock of the fucking walk. I didn't give a fuck about anyone in the prison or anything like that. As far as I was concerned, there was no point in being a nice guy when you ended up in prison. The other inmates would stand on your fucking head if they had half the chance. It's the law of the jungle; kill or be killed.

I became even more twisted. I blamed my father for what happened. He should have told the police that he found the bike instead of walking me into it. It didn't matter to me anyway.

Although Upton screwed my mind, I think St. Patrick's in Dublin made me physically dangerous.

When I started boxing, I learned how to do real damage with my fists.

The hatred I felt for authority got worse. I became very violent, I attacked screws [prison officers] and got locked up more times than anyone else. A week didn't pass without me being banned from the recreation room at night. I didn't care. If they couldn't break me inside Upton, there was no way St. Patrick's could. The place was a holiday camp compared to Upton.

While I was in St. Patrick's, my family moved from Sheriff Street to Keogh Square, which was an old army barracks in Inchicore. The only people who lived there were people who didn't pay their rent on time to Dublin Corporation. The people of Keogh Square were real Dubliners; they were genuine people; they would help you any way they could. I remember this woman that lived up the road from our flat. Her name was Mrs. Doyle. If my Ma had no money, she could go in there, borrow Mr. Doyle's suit, pawn it and get it back out on Friday. If Mrs. Doyle had no money, she came down and got Da's suit and she'd do the same thing. The people of Keogh Square didn't have much but they were willing to share what little they had.

My spell in Borstal had made me hungry for women. When I was released, I started running wild once again. There was no better place to learn sex education than Inchicore. I started knocking about with a married woman. I'd go up to her flat and she showed me things I never thought possible. She was fun but she was too old. I wanted to practise on someone younger than me. I started going out with a girl called *Bríde*. I thought I loved her. You think you love people, but you don't really love them at all.

It was a fairly heavy relationship. I think we spent the whole relationship having it off but she was the first woman to ever hurt me. I was out one night in Keogh Square and I caught her two-timing me.

There were no lights in the stairwells of the flats in those days. I was going home one night when I heard this little giggle in the hall. I knew that giggle. When I went to investigate, I saw her with two guys and they were tearing her out of it. So much for that relationship.

I went out with another girl after her. That was a nightmare. Her family were all Travellers and her father didn't really like the look of me. No prizes for guessing what way that ended up.

I then met another girl. Her name was Patricia Wynn. She was about three years younger than I was; I think she was 14-years-old.

She was the most beautiful girl in the world. She was pretty and there was something about her smile. We just clicked. I called her Lobbins.

We started going out together. We had the time of our lives. I think everyone spends some part of his or her life not caring about what other people think. Lobbins made me forget about Upton and the memories. She made me forget about my troubles. You see, Lobbins had this calming effect on me. I still can't tell you what was special about her but she just had this quality.

We were going out together for about a year when I got caught by the law. I was sentenced to three years for a robbery. I couldn't believe it. I was heartbroken.

I was never one of these prisoners who complained when they were locked up. Don't get me wrong, I was violent and aggressive towards anyone who pissed me off. If any person tried to bully me I would kick them unconscious. I didn't care who they were. If you wanted trouble, I was your man.

I threw myself back into boxing in St. Patrick's. I did my best to forget about Lobbins and put her out of my mind; there was no point in trying to keep the romance going when I knew I could never be with her. Her family didn't want her to go near me. I suppose I took the view that she would meet someone else. Who fucking cared anyway? I didn't expect anyone to remain loyal to me. That made it easier for me to be disloyal to them.

Life was going along as normal, if you can call prison life normal, when I got an unexpected visit. I was called out to a visitor's room where Lobbins's father and my Da were waiting.

Front row, second from left: I often look at this photograph in wonder and wish I could start my life again. This photograph shows me in Upton where I was subjected to unspeakable acts of cruelty.

Socialising: Lila and myself step out for the first time.

Lobbins didn't deserve the life I gave her. She derserved much better.

Bo Bo the charmer.

4

Patrick , and 22/11/1961

24. ST Bridgets Gardens

North Wall Dublin

Sir,

I wish to make my application to your Offices on behalf of my Son Maurice who is at Present Detained in Cork Industrial School. he was sent away on the 9/1/1956 for taking a Prayer Book and for none attendance of School. he had never been in any other trouble and been so far away, I was hoping that you would consider his case and be so good as to have him released for the Coming Christmas as he will be 16 on the 24 March coming, so if Sir you could take these couple of Months of his detention and let him home for Christmas, I Patrick Ward as well as my whole Family will be very grateful to you and your good offices your Humble Servant

Patrick Ward

Larry doesn't carry: Larry Dunne pumped heroin into Dublin. Much to my shame, I got involved with his dealers and the drugs trade. It's not something I'm very proud of.

The General: Martin Cahill was a diamond. He used to come over to my house and ask for advice about bank robberies. I was sad when the IRA whacked him.

John Gilligan: I thought John was dead on until he got involved in the drugs trade. When I was a member of the Warehouse Gang I believed he was the best robber of his generation. He was a master criminal and well respected in the underworld until he was linked to Veronica Guerin's murder.

Tommy Coyle: Slippery as an eel, my good old friend Tommy Coyle. He was a master conman, fence and drug dealer.

Paul 'Hippo' Ward: Hippo became a member of Gilligan's drugs gang, after I left the Warehouse Gang. He used to give me a couple of grand when times were hard.

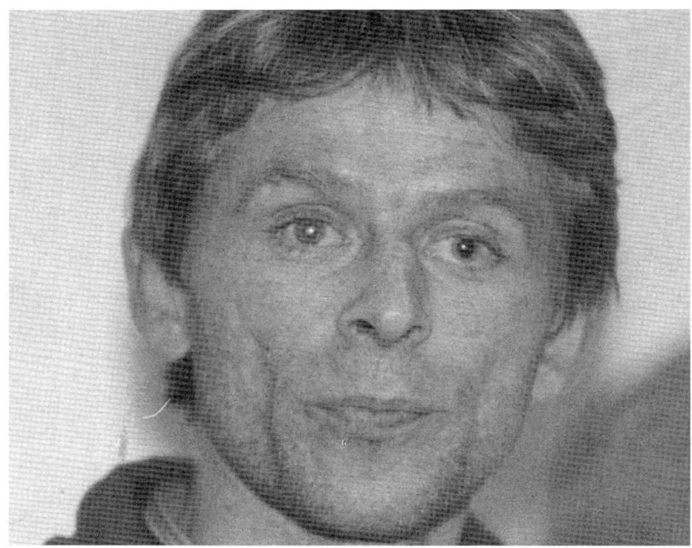

Declan Griffin: Griffin was one of the main drug dealers targeted by the anti-drugs movement. I threatened to murder him every second day of the week but he wouldn't stop pushing drugs.

Marven Hagler: I've met a few famous people during my time. Here I am with Marven Hagler, boxing legend.

John Kelly: Here I am with John Kelly of Survivors of Child Abuse (SOCA). John is a top guy and a good friend of mine. He has fought to get justice for men like me. I've nothing but respect for him.
© *Photocall Ireland*

This is me with my boy, Lance. I hope my children never lead the life that I have led. I hope this book teaches them what their Da was really like and why I became what I was.

I knew immediately that Lobbins was pregnant; I knew by the way her father, Jack, looked at me. Part of me felt my world collapsing; the other part of me felt delighted. I suppose it is also true to say I didn't know what to feel.

Jack came straight to the point. He asked me what I was going to do about it. I will always remember his face when I said, 'Sure what can I do about it, I'm in doing three years, do you know what I mean?'

Back in those days, when you got a girl pregnant, you either got married or the girl went to a home for unmarried mothers. There was no question of that happening but Jack didn't want me near her. He said I was nothing but trouble.

Da told me I had to do the right thing, which kind of made me smile. He said he was going to talk to the social welfare officer in the prison about a wedding. I told him not to say a word but he wouldn't listen.

'This is more important than your pride, Bo Bo.'

I didn't want anyone to know my business and Jack was going mad. That's why I told him to keep his mouth shut. I told Da the social welfare officers couldn't keep anything to themselves. But there was no room for discussion with my Da. I think he was more excited than me. He went off for about an hour and came back to tell me they'd sort something out.

I'd asked Lobbins to visit me but Jack wouldn't let her see me. Then she turned up. Fuck, she looked young. I knew by looking at her that she was afraid.

She was only a child. She should have been out playing with dolls, not visiting me in prison. This was not the life she wanted. This was a fucking disaster. Our families started making plans but needless to say I had no input because I was locked up.

About three months later, Da came and told me I was getting married in a week's time. He said the prison officers were going to let me out for a day under escort.

The wedding would take place in St. Michael's Church beside Keogh Square. Da said the priest knew the score. The governor then came to me and said he'd let me sit with my new wife in the car.

'You and her can have a little chat and when your wife comes up to see you that day, we'll give you an extra visit on top of the one you normally get. Instead of a half an hour, we will give you an hour or an hour and a half. How about that, Bo Bo?'

I thought they were all fucking mad. I was shitting myself. This was crazy.

The day finally came and I was brought to the church by a screw we called Harry.

Harry was all right; he wasn't the worst. He would never give you trouble for the sake of it. Harry let us do our own thing. The prisoners never caused him trouble because he treated us with respect. If someone did start messing with Harry, he would be told to stop by the prisoners.

On the day of my wedding, Harry took me out of the prison with another two screws. Getting married was the strangest thing that ever happened to me. Everyone remembers the day they get married but I spent the rest of my life trying to forget it. I don't regret marrying Lobbins; I regret the way it happened. She made a serious mistake getting married to me.

The screws came and took me out of my cell. They said they had to handcuff me. I was already shitting myself so this only made me more nervous. When they put me in the car, they told me they couldn't take off the cuffs even though I promised I wouldn't make a run for it.

When I got to the church I asked Harry to take the handcuffs off and he told me he couldn't, he'd have to leave them on.

'For fucks sake Harry, I'm getting married. I can't get married with cuffs.'

'I've no choice, Bo Bo. I'm sorry.'

After some serious talk, he said okay. I went into the church with the two screws watching. Harry stood at the back of the church. I knew he was mortified.

I was standing there. I was shitting myself. Then I heard the music.

Lobbins came into the church. There was no pomp and ceremony. They rushed her up the altar and the priest read out the wedding rites as quickly as he could. And that was it.

There were no hugs. There were no kisses. There was no honeymoon. There was no romance.

I came out of the church and I was chained once again to the screws. I couldn't even cuddle Lobbins. I didn't know what to think.

When I said Harry was okay, I meant it. When they put me back into the car, Harry asked Lobbins to sit in beside me and he drove us down the road. He pulled up outside a shop, then stepped out and left the two of us sitting there alone. That was Harry's way. He was trying to be nice.

Harry then bought the two of us a bottle of Coca-Cola and a little cake. We broke it in half and shared it. I didn't know what to say to her. She was devastated. This was not what she wanted. No girl wants to get married like this.

We sat in the back of the car and made the best of the situation. I talked about the baby coming along. I told her to make sure she visited later that day because they were giving me a special visit. She promised she would come. I told her that if she didn't come, I would be left there waiting for hours.

When we finished the drinks, Harry apologised and said I had to get back to St. Patrick's. He dropped Lobbins back to the church where her family was waiting. I waved goodbye.

When I was brought back to St. Patrick's, the other guys were giving me loads of stick, which is only natural. The screws took me out of my cell to wait on Lobbins but she never came.

I was left waiting there for hours. I swore to myself that I would never trust her again. And I never trusted her again. I now realise she was only a young girl trapped in a nightmare but I didn't see it that way at the time. She did come to visit the next day but it didn't matter.

I was married about four months when I appealed my sentence. I got out in time for the birth of the baby. We called her Tina. I will never forget how beautiful she looked in the hospital. I remember I was just out of prison and seeing this little thing in a load of clothes; she was so small, so tiny, so fragile.

I was over the moon. I felt like a real man. I felt great despite the fact we were poor. At the time, we couldn't afford our own home so we moved in with my Ma and Da. There wasn't much room in her flat so Lobbins and I slept on an old settee; the baby slept in the pram beside us.

I knew the moment we moved in with my parents that we wouldn't be staying long. My parent's flat was too small. I eventually had an argument with Da about something, I don't know what it was, but I'll never forget leaving.

It was snowing that night and he told me to get the fuck out. I called him a fucking bastard and walked out. He then called me back and said to me, 'Take them two with you as well.'

He was talking about Lobbins and Tina. I never forgave him for that.

We took refuge with Lobbins's mother. She lived at the archway near Keogh Square. I explained what had happened when we arrived at the front door. Mrs. Wynn was kind enough to give us the box room. Lobbins's family were decent people; they had nothing but they did the best they could.

I had no money and no job. I had a wife and baby to feed.

I felt I had no option but to start robbing again. I don't mean robbing houses around Keogh Square or anything like that, I mean I started robbing banks.

chapter eight

I should explain what I mean when I say I got heavily involved in organised crime. I believe there are two types of criminal. The first type is the petty criminal. They occasionally commit a crime when they get the opportunity. They might buy stolen goods when they are going cheap. You don't need me to tell you there are people out there who will buy anything once it's going cheap. They might sell a few ecstasy tablets or porno videos to make a few quid on the side. I was a petty criminal when I was five-years-old.

I became the second type of criminal when I reached my late teens. I became what you would call a professional; or a gangster. People like me gradually come to think about nothing but crime; we make our living from criminality. In simple terms, we are the people that sell drugs to addicts, break into homes and factories, and shoot anyone who gets in our way. We all deny this but that's what we are like. We need guns to protect ourselves and we spend our lives being watched by the gardaí.

I had flirted on the edge of organised crime since I was a boy but I never got involved. All that changed when I came out of Borstal. The people I mixed with were hard men who used guns. They introduced me to extreme violence.

When I turned 19 years of age, I was recruited into what was Ireland's first gang. They were safe breakers. Two brothers ran the firm. I won't name them but let's just say that one was tall while the other was short.

Safes were easy to open in those days. They were like wooden boxes with metal fronts. They were designed to protect money and documents from fires – not to protect hard cash from professional thieves.

You might ask why the brothers wanted me to join them. It was simple. I could break into any house or factory with little or no effort. I had a reputation for squeezing into small holes and through windows. I could get into buildings that no one else could. And I was fucking fearless. I was afraid of nothing. If we happened to come across someone, I would think nothing of punching his or her head in. I wouldn't give it a second thought. Didn't give a fuck.

Within weeks of my release I robbed about four factories with this crew. The one job that sticks out in my mind most involved a factory off Moore Street in Dublin city.

The factory made fluffy stuff for packaging. I can't remember what it was called. The two brothers knew there was a safe in the personnel department and told me to find a way in.

I duly obliged. I scouted the area looking for an access point. I mingled among the market traders and shoppers on Moore Street. Nobody noticed me. I was wandering about looking at the roof and side windows but I could find no chink in the armour. Then I noticed a fire escape attached to a fish shop down the street. It was one of those ladders you pull down.

Here was my backdoor. I went back that same evening and pulled down the ladder with a bit of wire. Up I went and across the roofs and on the factory's roof.

As soon as I saw the owners locking up, I went in through a skylight.

I was fucking great. There was no stopping me; I loved robbing. The exhilaration was better than sex. I can't begin to tell you what it was like dropping into the factory. It made the blood rush through my veins.

Once I was inside, I made my way downstairs and opened up the backdoor where the brothers were now waiting. I gave three knocks from inside the door and waited for four knocks back. That was a code we used.

Knock . . . Knock. . . Knock.

'It's us, Bo Bo.'

I swung the door open.

'That's our boy.'

'You were supposed to knock four times.'

'Hurry up, Bo Bo. We have no time for trick-acting.'

Years of thieving had trained the brothers to operate in total darkness. They could find their way around in the dark. They were like cats.

The brothers taught me never to switch on lights. They attracted attention but also helped witnesses identify you if they stumbled upon you.

I remember standing there when they got to work on the safe. It was my first real heist.

The taller one walked into the room and opened up a canvas bag that contained his tools. Shorty was busy looking at the safe.

I thought they were real professionals. The tall brother handed a jemmy-bar to the short brother. Shorty wedged the jemmy-bar in between the hinges and the door. The tall brother then picked up another jemmy-bar and did the same. These guys were all about brute force. When the jemmy-bars were in place, Shorty got a lump hammer from the bag and walloped the back of the safe.

It was fucking amazing. The whole thing fell apart.

When the dust settled, I could see money everywhere. It was more money than I'd seen in my life. It was fucking unreal.

I stood there like a fucking fool while the brothers stuffed the money into the bag. I didn't count it. We headed out the back door and off we went.

The two brothers were clever pricks. They never counted the money in front of me. Looking back on it now it is obvious they were fleecing me but I didn't see it that way.

I would usually get around £100 for each job. That was serious cash in those days. The money allowed me to enjoy women and that was all I cared about. That factory was one of the first that I hit. I did a few more jobs with the two brothers but I fell out with them over money.

While this was going on, I was the worst husband in the world. I abandoned Lobbins to crime and womanising. When I did a job, I used to pick up a bird and head off for a few days. Anything in a skirt; it didn't matter what she looked like, just as long as she did what she was told.

I would fuck anyone but my wife. I would love them and leave them, and then go home. Then I'd go back out again. I lived the fast life. I never spent the money I made on anything of value.

I never opened a bank account. I never went into a bank to put money in although I went into a bank and took money out, if you know what I mean.

That is why I never had money. I spent all my cash on birds. I still meet guys to the present day, who I stroked with. They say to me, 'Jaysus Bo Bo, you must be loaded.'

My response has always been the same. How could I be loaded if every slut in Dublin was looking like a lady. I spent every penny I robbed on women.

I used to meet girls in the pubs. I would take them out and buy them something; a dress or maybe a bottle of perfume. I would let them think I was in love with them. In my defence there were only certain birds I would do it with. The rest were just cheap birds who would ride anyone.

No matter how much money I made it wasn't enough. I spent every single penny on boozing and women. I gave nothing to my family. I let my children go without clothes and food. I left my wife to fend for herself.

I was fairly well-known in the Dublin crime scene by the time I reached my twenties. Gangs across the city wanted me to join them. I had a great reputation for violence and everyone knew I would never give the game away if I was caught by the gardaí. I'd rather slit my own throat; this made me a good fella to work with.

Wealth is addictive. I needed money to sustain the fast women and lifestyle I wanted. Money gave me power.

I started working with a guy called O'Brien. He's dead now. He was one clever bastard. He came up with the idea of robbing branches of the Saxone shoe shops.

He never said, but I believe he had inside information on cash collections and deliveries. He used to drive me around the country just to rob the shoe shops.

We made a bundle – enough to choke a horse. O'Brien would collect me and another guy on Sheriff Street and take us to towns in the Midlands. Robbing those shops was like taking sweets from a baby. The money was just left in the till. In those days I just kicked in the back door of the shop, walked through the storeroom and nicked the cash from the till.

I made about £800 from the scam, which was big money. Put it this way, I could have bought a brand new mini for £375 or a house for £500 at the time.

There was no stopping me. I had a great life. I lived in hotels; I slept with different women every week and I didn't give a fuck about anyone.

The shoe shop scam ran for about two months before the gardaí caught up with me.

This particular copper got hold of my name and I got pulled. I remember the day they moved on me. I was standing at the door of a place called the Rainbow Café on O'Connell Street. This was a very famous place. Every thief in Dublin would hang out there.

It was a den of sleaze. Robbers and safe crackers would all hang out there during the day. The young prostitutes used the Rainbow at night. It was a place where people like me could meet up and chat.

The moment I was lifted, the Rossers raided my Da's home. I had just given him a couple of hundred pounds. When the bastards searched the house, they found the money and asked Da where it came from.

They brought the two of us to the Bridewell Station where I was interviewed by these two coppers.

I kept saying that I didn't know anything about the shoe shop raids and I kept asking them why they had arrested my Da.

'He doesn't rob. He's worked all of his life.'

'We know that, Bo Bo. We know you gave him the money. Why don't you admit it?'

'Jesus, lads you've got this wrong. He saved the money. He's a worker. He's worked all his life.'

I knew I was fucked. They knew everything. Where would my Da get a few hundred pounds?

They then produced a jemmy-bar they had found in one of the shops we raided. I said I'd never seen it before. We used to leave the jemmy-bars behind instead of carrying them with us. After the job, it was out for some booze and capture some bird and that was it. We never thought about leaving evidence behind.

'Really, Bo Bo. We know it's you. You're going down Bo Bo.'

I said nothing. They took me out of the interview room and sneered at me. I got 18 months, which was nothing given what I had been up to. I remember speaking to one of the Rossers on the day I was being taken away to prison.

'You know you bastard, I didn't do this.'

He said to me, 'We know that you did do it. But you are not going down for something you've done. You're going down for all of the things that you got away with.'

What could I say?

I became bitter enemies with some gardaí. They did everything they could to stop me. The biggest trick they ever pulled was letting Lobbins know that I was fucking around behind her back.

I remember one particular day when the Rossers raided my gaff in Keogh Square. I came to the bedroom door only to be met by this copper. I knew the fella well. He could see Lobbins standing behind me.

'Is that your wife?'

'Yeah, why?'

'That's funny, because when I raided a house in Buckingham Street last week, you were in bed with a blonde.'

The bastard then told Lobbins that I had not one, but dozens of women. He told her I was a scumbag. He went further. He told her I went down the country for dirty weekends while she was stuck with the children.

He was one hundred percent right but I couldn't admit to anything. I was a slut. I was an out and out fucking slut. As much as I hate to admit it, I kind of enjoyed the fact that everyone knew I was sleeping around.

I learned valuable lessons when I set out on the path to organised crime. I learned it was important to hold down a job if possible so you could explain where you got money from.

The sad thing is that I had some great jobs but never gave them any commitment. I didn't care. I could make easy money robbing. I learned to be a steeplejack with Irish Engineering. I spent five years working with them. It was great. You would get an hour off for dinner but I used the time to rob houses.

No one wanted me to go straight. They preferred to see me out robbing because they got a few quid out of me.

I also worked with Dublin Corporation. My job was opening and locking four gates down at the fruit market. It was a great job. But I couldn't settle down.

At one stage, Dublin Corporation put me in charge of collecting money from the Ivy market, the fish market and the cattle market. I used to collect the money every week. One day I decided I would organise a few of the guys to rob my own office. I got the lads to go ahead of me and collect the money.

When I arrived to make my collection, there was no money because one of my mates had already collected it. To cover my tracks, I rang the office.

'Listen, the girls up here are telling me that the money has already been collected.'

'How could that be Maurice?'

'How the fuck do I know? Did you send someone up?'

'No.'

'Well, ring the other places around there and see if their boxes have been collected. I think that someone has been watching me going around collecting. They must know my route and have gone and collected the boxes before me.'

The boss told me to come back to the yard at once. When I arrived, he told me that all the cash boxes had been collected and the gardaí were on their way. He said I would have to give a statement to the police. I said I had no problem with that.

A team of gardaí came down from the Bridewell Station. Every one of the fuckers knew me as a criminal. I could see them grinning and laughing when they were talking to the boss. They kept pointing over in my direction. I had a fair idea what they were saying.

The boss then came out to me. He said the gardaí seemed to know me. I acted all defensive.

'What do you mean by that?'

'The police seem to think that you have got something to do with this.'

'What do you think?'

'I know you would never do anything like that Maurice. You have been doing this job for two years, and nothing like this ever happened before. Plus, the girls said it wasn't you that went up to them and collected the money.

'Whatever you say, I stand with you. I have already told the police that. I told them that I didn't think it was you.'

I thought he was a fucking thick but he knew all along it was me. When I arrived for work the following Monday, the boss transferred me to the cattle market.

I couldn't do anything. There was no point in complaining. I went up to the cattle market and was met by the foreman. He gave me a hose and a spade, and told me to sweep up the cow shit. I chucked the shovel at him – I said he could shove his job up his bollocks.

I didn't want his fucking job. I left. I didn't care because I had made £1,500 from the robbery.

chapter nine

When I lost my job with Dublin Corporation I decided to move to Wales for a few months until the fuss died down. Some of the people from Keogh Square used to go abroad for the summer to work in hotels during the tourist season. I decided to go with them.

I abandoned Lobbins and the children. I was so screwed up in the head that I didn't give a shit about them. I cared about nothing or no one. There was no big goodbye or anything like that. As far as I was concerned, I was just getting offside. I never thought about the effects this would have on my children. I am now ashamed of what I did and the cruel life I gave to Lobbins.

I travelled with a friend of mine called *Andy* to the town of Llandudno in Wales. It was the first time I travelled abroad. We went from the North Wall to Holyhead and then from Holyhead to Llandudno.

We got jobs in a place called the Armscliff Hotel. I had two jobs actually. The manager gave me a job in the ice cream shop.

I was officially an ice cream chef. That sounds very high and mighty but it just involved dishing out the ice cream.

My second job was cleaning shoes. All the residents would leave their shoes outside the doors every night. My job was to collect them using a trolley, take them away, polish them and bring them back.

It was a shit job but the people who owned the hotel were very good. They liked the Irish.

I came to like Llandudno. It was like home from home because there were always a few Dubliners working in the kitchens.

I lived in a chalet in a field at the back of the hotel, which quickly turned into a hang out for women. We all used to party in the fields around the chalet. I called the place 'Happy Valley' because I used to go there with the local girls.

I know you are probably asking yourself what sort of bastard I was. The truth is that I didn't really care about responsibilities. I slept with a dozen women in Wales. I said earlier I was going to be honest. Well, I'm telling it like it is.

I never once thought about my wife or children. I didn't send them money. I blew it on women.

The local girls thought the Irish boys were great because we got everything for free. My mates used to work on the carnival rides so I would bring the women for rides, then back to the hotel for more of the same.

I won't say I tried to steer away from crime but I didn't do anything for a few months. I didn't even look at lifting a wallet from the Armscliff. But temptation always came my way. This time temptation came in the form of a vulnerable safe.

I was on my rounds one night when I saw a porter putting wads of cash into the safe, which was under the desk in the reception area.

I couldn't resist it. I told *Andy* I was going to have a go that same night. He decided to join me. We had a brief chat about how good the hotel had been to us and the Irish working over there, but we said fuck the lot of them. That was my attitude. The one thing we did promise was not to use violence.

I didn't put any great planning into the robbery. There was a guy on the reception area that night. We simply strolled into the lobby and told the porter to take a break.

'Thanks boys. That's really kind of you. I'll be back in a jiffy.'

Once the porter walked out of the room, *Andy* and I got on our hands and knees. I took a closer look at the safe. I had opened ones like it before when I worked with Shorty and Tall.

I told *Andy* to grab one end of the safe and lift. We managed to get it off the ground and onto the reception desk. It weighed a ton.

There was a building site next door to the hotel. Back in those days, workmen left their tools lying around because no one robbed. Well, most people didn't rob.

I told *Andy* to lift the safe out through the side door. The two of us lifted the safe out, then threw it over a small wall and dumped it on some waste ground. The safe landed with a bang. *Andy* stood there keeping watch while I ran off and got a pickaxe and a few bars.

Bang.

'Don't hit it so hard, Bo Bo. You'll wake everyone up.'

Bang.

The second blow knocked it open. The pickaxe had caused the safe to crack open at the back. I stuck my hand inside and started feeling about.

It didn't take me long to locate the cash. I pulled one bundle of notes out. I found another one. Then I found some pieces of jewellery. There was about £1000 altogether. We were fucking loaded.

But there was no time to celebrate. We went straight back to the chalet and got this Irish guy who had a car to drive us up to Birmingham. We gave him £100 to keep his mouth shut. *Andy* had friends in Birmingham so we moved in with them. We figured the cops would be searching everywhere for us.

This was a major robbery. This was £1000 which at the time could have bought two houses.

Remember what I said when I told you that the more money you have, the more money you spend? We blew the money in four weeks but those weeks were memorable. *Andy* and myself had the time of our lives.

I always believed that criminals rob to sustain their lifestyles. Anyone who gets used to blowing £1000 on women, boozing and clothes, finds it hard to start living a normal life. I suppose if I am brutally honest with myself, I didn't want to live a normal life. Why would I want to look after my family and scrape along, when I could party every night and sleep with loads of women?

That was my logic. *Andy* was the same. So we decided to do something else to raise a few quid. I scouted Birmingham and decided to rob a branch of Burtons just off the King's Road. This was an easy job. There were no alarms in those days so it was just a matter of breaking into the shop and nicking some of the clobber.

The shop was located below a block of apartments. These provided an extra opportunity to raise some cash. I went upstairs, checked to see if there was anyone at home, then riddled them. I got some nice jewellery in one of the flats, which I gave to *Andy*. You might think that we left Birmingham as quick as possible after doing Burtons but we didn't. I was reckless. When I say I didn't give a fuck about what happened, I mean it. We changed into the clothes we had stolen and went to the local pub called the Moth Shovel on the Coventry Road. We got pissed out of our heads that night.

I think everyone makes a stupid decision at some point but I can't say I made many correct decisions in my life. I never really thought about the future or what was coming down the road. I think I spent my life trying to erase the memories of my past.

I think it was for this reason that I never really thought things through. The day after the Burtons robbery, I decided to go back to Llandudno. I don't know what was going through my mind but *Andy* and myself got the train to Wales.

Llandudno was a large enough town. I didn't think anyone would recognise me because there were so many Irish people working there.

I decided to give crime a break for a while so I got a job as a lift operator in Carrolls Hotel. I was there for about three days when I was arrested. I was standing in the hotel lobby when I saw a couple of policemen walk in. I thought something had happened in the hotel but they were looking for me.

They arrested me in front of everyone and brought me to the local police station. Once I was inside the interrogation room, they started asking me about the safe. I knew I was fucked. They knew everything about me.

'We already have your friend in custody,' said one of them.

I knew the game was over. I asked them what evidence they had against me, only to hear that everyone I worked with had made statements about me. As I said earlier, the owners of the Armscliff Hotel were good to their Irish staff. When I stole the money from the safe, it wasn't the Welsh people who were angry; it was the Irish. I got two years inside Waltham Prison for the robbery.

The main thing I remember about that jail sentence was the two queers I met inside the prison. It was the first time I had ever seen two homosexuals – two fucking real life queers. I was amazed at these guys. They were like girls.

I met them when I was walking along the landing to the governor's parade. I thought they were two girls. This fella who was with me poked me in the arm and said, 'Look at them.'

I couldn't believe my eyes. The two of them started waving at me and blowing me kisses.

'Those guys are real queers.'

Then one of them shouted over, 'Hi honey. If you need anyone to do any washing love you know where I am.'

Was this a fucking joke or what? The whole parade fell around laughing. They were two queers all right but they were actually nice fellas. They were young guys but boy, were they feminine. One of them had long hair like a bird. He wore a shirt tied in a knot to show off his belly. When he walked he had a waggle. I was amazed.

I couldn't believe there were people like that. When I heard people talking about blokes dressing up as women, I thought it was a load of shit.

I was placed in the youth wing. I was only allowed out for an hour each day; half an hour in the morning and half an hour in the evening.

It was my first time in an English prison but it was exactly the same as Ireland. The accents were different, but the screws were a bit more vicious than an Irish prison. In Ireland, if you didn't fuck with them, they wouldn't fuck with you.

The English screws would attack you no matter what. I shared a cell with two coloured guys but they were the biggest racists I ever met. They asked me where I was from on the first day. When I said Dublin, they stopped talking to me. I usually couldn't care less about who talked to me but when you are sharing a cell it's a problem.

They wouldn't talk to me at all. They talked to each other in their own language. I knew I had to get out of the cell, and the best and quickest way to get out was to mill them.

They maintained the silence for a few days and only spoke to me when they had to. I decided there was only one way I was going to sort this out.

I had absolutely nothing over there because I had no family near me. I couldn't even afford the price of a cigarette. My two brothers on the other hand had plenty; they had cigarettes, sweets and newspapers.

After about five days, I asked the two of them if I could have their butts. One of the two was smoking a cigarette.

I used to put tea leaves on a radiator pipe and dry them out. I smoked the tea leaves because I had no money to buy real tobacco. I had fuck all over there. Nobody was sending me anything.

The black fucker said nothing to me. He just kept smoking the cigarette. When he finished his last drag, he threw the butt into the piss pot.

I said nothing and just stared at him. This bastard thought he was a real smart guy.

'What's your fucking problem? We are all fucking prisoners, and we should all work together.'

He laughed at me and smiled at his mate. That was his biggest mistake; he didn't see me coming.

If you ever have to use violence against someone always wait for the person to relax. Winning a fight is all about timing. The trick is to wait until your victim thinks you are not going to do anything and has relaxed. It's impossible to make anyone who has adrenaline pumping through their veins feel pain. Adrenaline numbs their senses. Once this fella thought the danger period was over, I fucking milled him.

He had just smiled at his friend when I landed a punch on his face. I beat that fucker black and blue.

He had these tribal scars on his face. I inflicted more. I held him with one hand and kept punching him in the face until he started spitting blood. When his friend tried to stop me, I caught him by the throat and knocked his two front teeth out.

Whenever I wanted to do serious damage to someone I always imagined I was beating Br. Buglar to death.

I left the two of them in a mess. The prison wardens arrived too late to save the cunts; the brothers were spitting out teeth and everything by the time they got the door open.

The governor moved me to another cell that night, which suited me fine. He asked me what had happened and I told him. I think he actually believed I was right to beat them because he never punished me.

There were very few Irish people in the prison at the time. There was a screw from Northern Ireland called McKenna. He was okay or rather he was the best out of a bad bunch. The blacks were the only people who racially abused me over there. No one ever gave me any trouble apart from the blacks. I think I was about four or five months into my sentence when a prison officer told me to get my kit ready.

'Where am I going?'

'You will know when you get there.'

He brought me down to the reception area where I got dressed. I had one of those Beatle suits with no collars and a pair of winkle pickers, the real pointy shoes.

I was sitting there waiting to be transferred when they brought me out to the gate where I saw two blokes waiting for me. I knew they were detectives just by looking at them. I thought they were arresting me for the Burtons robbery but I said nothing.

'What prison are we going to?'

'You are not going to any prison. You are being deported.'

'What?'

They explained that my trial judge had ordered that I be released after five months. The detectives said I had to sign a form promising that I wouldn't enter Britain for ten years.

I said that wasn't a problem and scribbled my name on some form. They had even bought me a plane ticket.

I arrived in Dublin Airport that same night where I was met by two coppers. They were there just to verify that I had arrived home.

I had no way of getting back to Keogh Square. I hadn't a penny in my pocket so I asked the two gardaí for a lift.

'Any chance of giving me a lift?'

'Make your own fucking way home.'

'I'll walk. But if I see anything on the way home, I'll have it and I'll get myself a taxi.'

True to my word I walked to Swords village, which was about three miles away, robbed a few shops and nicked some money, which I used to pay for my taxi home.

chapter ten

Armed robbery is like gambling. They can both make you instantly rich but they can also go wrong. If you get caught for armed robbery, you're looking at ten years in prison. If someone gets shot and wounded, you get life. The rewards are high but so are the risks.

I got involved in three armed robberies when I returned from Britain. I regret the day I got involved in any of them. I nearly shot a guy who tried to overpower me and I beat him so badly that he was in a coma for a week. He's lucky I didn't kill him.

At the time I didn't care because I made a small fortune but looking back I now feel ashamed. I was a fucking animal; I was a dangerous bastard.

In those days, I knew every single criminal godfather in Dublin. I worked on a freelance arrangement with them. If they were short of a man they would come to me and ask if I was interested in some work. Some of the major crime bosses would simply come and ask for my advice.

The General was a regular visitor to my door. I thought Martin Cahill was a fucking diamond. I never did any work with him but he often came down to the house just to ask me about certain things. Did I see this, did I see that? I would give him my thoughts.

Martin liked me because I was a loner. He'd also been through the industrial school system so he knew the score. He liked the fact I would hit seven or eight places a day and make easy money. Martin respected me for that. He knew I needed no one for backup.

I did my first armed robbery with a major crime gang during the early Seventies. I won't give a specific date because the cops would arrest me.

Every garda in the country will know the guys I am talking about but I won't mention their names. The boss asked me to come on board. I had done some work with him before but nothing involving guns; just break-ins. I liked the way he worked; I thought the boss was bang on.

He approached me while I was having a drink in Bartley Dunne's pub with some slut one night. He walked into the bar and nodded at me. I got rid of the tart and brought him over to a quiet corner where we sat down to have a more private chat. He told me he was planning a job. It was against a company on the south quays.

'Do you fancy the work, Bo Bo?'

We referred to armed robbery as work. Crime paid our wages. I readily agreed because I was always interested in making money.

The gang met up the next day to finalise the plans. I drove down to the quays and had a good look myself. It seemed a simple enough job. The biggest problem we faced was the getaway, but the boss said he had that covered.

After a few days, we all gathered together to carry out the job. The plan was as follows: three of us would go in while the getaway driver waited outside.

My job was to overpower the security guard and hold him in a small office to the left of the door.

The guns we planned to use for the job belonged to the boss. He had his own arsenal; everybody in the underworld knew that.

But I had a problem with this. The boss was a known liar. He would give you a shotgun or a handgun no problem, but he was known to hand out guns with no bullets. I recall that bullets were hard to get back in those days.

I could see his logic. Whenever he was caught doing this he would say he was protecting the team. If you were on a stroke and something happened, he knew that no one could get murdered if the team didn't have a loaded gun. On the other hand, if something did go wrong, you were defenceless.

I told him out straight that if he tried any of that crap with me I'd blow his fucking head off. He said, 'Okay'.

The day before the job, he brought me down and showed me which building we were going to hit. He had found an escape route through a backdoor just in case things went wrong.

We hit the company at lunch-time the next day. We pulled up in the car and went straight in the front door. When we got just inside the door, I pulled a mask over my face.

I went in the door as planned and saw the little office on the left, where there was one young fella. I took him no problem and brought him up to the second floor. The two others had gone ahead of me with guns blazing.

We found someone else on the second floor, and we tied the two of them up together.

When one of the guys went to the office where the safe was hidden, he found a man and a woman in the room. When they saw us coming they shit themselves. The bloke opened the safe. He said he'd give us whatever we wanted but pleaded with us not to harm anyone.

There wasn't any bother. I just told him to open the safe and we took the money.

I had sent one guy back to the front door to deal with anyone who came in. He was told to tie them up and hold them in the room on the left. But he started losing his bottle.

The job was running like clockwork upstairs. The manager helped us fill about £20,000 into a sack. When the money was bagged, I headed down the stairs and went to jump into the getaway car with the others. But the boss asked me to make sure the hostages were tied up properly.

The next thing I heard was the sound of patrol cars. I didn't need anyone to tell me the gang were leaving me behind.

Fuck this.

I legged it out the door and pointed the sawn-off shotgun I was carrying at the getaway car. If they moved an inch I was going to blow the boss's head off. This all happened in a split second.

I dived into the car and we headed down to Grand Canal Quay. We parked the car on the side of the road and jumped into a van, which was waiting for us. The car and the van were from a garage. The boss had a friend who worked in a garage and gave us cars and vans during dinner hour. We always made sure to have the cars back on time.

No one said anything in the van. After about ten minutes of silence the boss said the job had went well. I pulled the gun on him and pointed it at his face.

'You fucking bastard! You were going to leave me there.'

'I wasn't, Bo Bo. I was only messing.'

'You fucking were, you cunt.'

I told him I believed him but I should have killed him there and then. I knew he was lying.

We decided to go to a restaurant to relax. If the cops were out searching for us they would never search the restaurants. When we had eaten our fill, we went to the Savoy cinema. We split the money inside the cinema. I don't know what was showing; I wasn't interested in what was on the screen.

I never worked with the gang after that. The boss came to me loads of times but I always said no. I didn't trust the fucker. I also didn't like the idea of having a gun in my hand. Believe it or not, I didn't think you had to have a gun in your hand when you went robbing – I just wasn't into it.

I actually never believed in it. You would get a colossal amount of time in prison if you were caught with a gun. When I broke into a house, the most I could get was twelve months. It was easy money.

I know the people I stole from were all victims and I feel bad about it now but it was all I could do to survive. There was nothing else I could do. It was either that or put birds on the game. There were a lot of guys I knew who lived off immoral earnings. I have no time for anyone who would do that type of thing. As far as I was concerned, any criminal who prostitutes women is lower than a screw, and you know what a screw is; he is a man who locks up another man every day.

The second armed robbery I set up involved a job on the Allied Irish Bank in Inchicore. Strangely enough, I organised the job after the bank helped my father.

This is what happened. A man came to our house and told my Da that he had won £300 on the St. Anthony's pools. He gave my Da a cheque and asked him to sign some form. He said there was a charge of £10 for the paperwork, which Da gave to him. £10 was a lot of money in those days but Da was over the moon with his win and went down to the bank to cash his cheque.

Da knew the bank manager very well so there was no problem with cashing the cheque. About three days later, the gardaí arrived at the door.

'Mr. Ward, I know that you have nothing to do with this, but that cheque you gave to the bank bounced – there was no such company. The cheque was a fake.'

Da was embarrassed because he knew the bank manager. He felt like a fucking fool because he believed he had won some money. Some chance. The next morning he went to the bank to say sorry for what had happened. He asked me to come along.

When we walked in the door, I saw this good-looking bird. I couldn't take my eyes off her. She went up to the bank manager and gave him a bag full of money. He emptied the bag on the table in front of me. There were blocks of cash. He signed a receipt and pushed the blocks through a hatch and put a little lock on the bag.

'Look at that pile of money, Da.'

'She comes in here every Tuesday, son.'

'It won't be there next fucking Tuesday.'

I remember the woman even to this day. She was a very sexy looking bird. She used to wear these little scarves and drove this little blue mini.

I got a three man team together to grab the bag the following Tuesday. It was like taking sweets from a child.

When she pulled in, I gave her about four or five minutes – then we hit her. I went into the bank armed with a shotgun. One of the guys with me had a hammer, and my other mate Francie had a big fucking blade.

When we ran into the bank, everyone hit the deck straight away so there were no problems.

The only guy who got a belt was the porter because he tried to be brave. He was about 50-years-old and we were in our twenties so I said he must be a fucking thrill seeker because he tried to have a go at Francie, who would have killed him.

There was no need to tie anyone up. The only things we did slam were the two front doors of the bank on the way out. I got £11,500 for that job.

The armed robbery I wish I had never done was on a pub. One of my mates worked in a bar and told me that the boss got extra money for the tills during bank holiday weekends. He also said the local workers used to cash their pay cheques in the pub.

He showed us the bank where his boss collected the money. He even showed us the route he took, where he parked his car and how he came in the back door to the pub when carrying cash.

The original plan was to hit him when he was coming out of the bank. But I said no. I believed we could get more money if we held him up inside the pub and forced him to open the safe. There were two others on the job with me and they both agreed.

I think we had watched him for about three months when we decided to strike. On the day in question, we waited for him to return from the bank before we went in after him.

We followed him back from the bank, watched him get out of his car and take the bag in with another bag and a couple of brown pouches. Everything was going according to plan. We caught him before he got inside the door to his office. I ran at him and pushed the door against him but I kind of fell on top of him. The two guys working with me ran into the bar and ordered the staff on the ground. There were no problems; so far so good. We locked all the doors.

The manager brought me into his office and opened the safe. So everything came together. There was a lovely buzz about the whole thing until one particular guy had a go at us.

When I was watching the money being counted, this guy jumped at me and knocked the gun out of my hand. He then punched me hard in the face.

We ended up fighting. I grabbed a big pole and I milled him with it. I kept clattering him with the pole. I beat him on the face. I almost knocked him unconscious. There was blood everywhere.

I was badly shaken. I picked up the gun and aimed at his head. I was going to shoot him. He had busted my lip.

I was looking at him. I told him to get on his hands and pray for mercy but he kept falling down. The others started screaming at me and pleading for mercy.

I couldn't understand why he tried to stop me robbing the place. It wasn't his money. It was his employer's money. I called him a fucking bastard.

'This money belongs to the fucking firm and you are only fucking labour. You don't own the money you bastard.'

I whacked him with the gun and I made my escape. I regret doing it but he deserved it. We weren't being heavy with him.

The robbery featured in the papers for about a week. The guy was unconscious for a few days in hospital. I have to admit I was frightened. I knew I had hurt the guy. But then, this fucker went for me. So I whacked him out of it. I think I would have killed him. That's what really frightened me. I knew if I was caught in a situation like that again, I wouldn't have any problem with killing a hostage.

I was never arrested for the robbery. I was pulled and questioned about it but I never appeared in court.

When the newspapers made a big deal of the beating, the gardaí were forced to act.

The papers printed descriptions of every one of us but the witnesses never got a good look at me because they said I was a skinhead. I never had a skinhead in my entire life.

Word spread like wildfire about the robbery. The cops knew within the space of a week that I was responsible.

I remember this old garda came to me and asked if he could have a word. I knew this garda. I always considered this fella to be a straight player. I went down to Kilmainham Garda Station. He brought me into a meeting room and sat me down. He said he knew that I was responsible. He actually said that I had went too far.

This cop was okay. He never raided your house. He would go to you and say 'I want to interview you', instead of dragging you out of bed. He would call up and tell me to come down to the station when he wanted to charge me. You knew exactly where you stood with a man like that.

When I heard him tell me I was going to get ten years I decided there and then that I would never do an armed robbery again.

That was the end of it for me. I was asked loads of times to help in armed robberies but I said no. If there were guns involved, I didn't want to know.

chapter eleven

I was jailed in 1972. I ended up doing 18 months for beating the shit out of a garda. I was sent to Mountjoy Prison, which was one of the hardest prisons in Europe. It was inside the Joy that I was first introduced to the IRA. They were housed in a wing called B2. I used to cut their hair.

Prisons are like communities with different prisoners fulfilling different functions. I was the barber, another guy would be a chef while another bloke would be the librarian.

I had the run of the prison. I could go anywhere I liked. But if you think I had it good, you should have seen the IRA set up.

They could bring in as much food as they wanted. When I used to visit B2, they even had tins of salmon.

I never had any Republican tendencies. I never saw the point of joining the IRA and robbing for them, and then giving them money. When I robbed, I robbed for myself. What few people realised is that most Republicans were mixed up with us. Some of them were even robbers.

I became very friendly with the lads jailed in B2. I'd arrive with my trolley and they would ask me to deliver a letter to such and such. I would also have to get the reply and bring it back.

As I said before, I never had any Republican tendencies but I respected the lads' right to fight for a United Ireland. I don't think any criminal felt otherwise, but the IRA came into conflict with me when they beat the living daylights out of two fellow prisoners called the Littlejohns.

These guys were jailed for a bank robbery but they were supposed to be undercover agents for MI5 or British Special Branch. They were supposedly sent to Ireland to try to infiltrate the IRA. If you ask me they were no more trying to penetrate the IRA than I was trying to penetrate Pamela Anderson.

They were here to make money. The brothers were housed in a double cell in the base alongside two UVF men. No prisoner talked to those two loyalist bastards. The Littlejohns wouldn't even talk to them.

But that didn't matter to the IRA. One morning, the republicans managed to get down into the base from

B2 and beat the brothers to within an inch of their lives. I went over to B2 afterwards and had a go at them. I said it was wrong; that these guys had milled the two Littlejohns for nothing.

I won't mention the IRA man's name but he basically told me to fuck off. He said the brothers were spies and should be executed.

I wasn't afraid of him. I told him that no one supported what they'd done.

'Youse are right pricks. Youse are right cunts for doing that.'

I was really annoyed because the Littlejohns had been cut badly. That was the end of the favours for a while. When they needed a haircut, I sent over the trimmer. They could do it themselves. As far as I was concerned, from now on they could fuck off.

I wasn't on speaking terms with the IRA for a while. You might wonder if I was scared. I wasn't. The IRA at the time didn't have the kind of clout in the underworld that they do today; they asked us for favours.

About a month later, one of the volunteers sent a message asking me for a meeting. This guy said the whole thing was a misunderstanding. He said a couple of fucking kids and hotheads had beaten the Littlejohns.

'You know the story, Bo Bo. You are a hothead yourself.'

This guy came from Ballybrack. I had known him since I was a boy. His father was very prominent in the IRA as well. I took what he said at face value and started cutting their hair again.

I was amazed when this guy was jailed for the IRA. He had been caught with batteries and some explosives. I didn't know he was involved until he ended up in the Joy.

I knew many of the senior fellas over the years. I met the IRA leader, Seán MacStioffan, a few times. He was a very quiet man; he kept to himself. He would only talk to you when he had something to say. He wouldn't try to make any conversation with you.

He was the first man I met in my entire life that could speak Irish. I have to say I was a bit paranoid. I would ask him if he was talking about me when I'd be trimming some guy's hair. I used to think he was talking about me when he was talking in Irish and the guys would start laughing.

'Jesus, Bo Bo. We are not saying anything about you.'

'If you are trying to make an eejit out of me, I'll show you who's the eejit.'

They would all start laughing and walk out. They could have wiped me out no problem.

I did a lot of running around for them, but I never read the letters or notes. I wouldn't even do that on an ordinary prisoner. Whatever was in their notes was nothing at all to do with me. I was getting well paid in cigarettes, tins of salmon and tins of fish.

To this day I am still amazed with the system they had going for themselves. They had everything brought in for them to eat; steak, chips and onions.

I have to say the IRA got up to some mad capers inside Mountjoy. They livened up the whole prison. I remember when MacStioffan went on hunger strike. They had to bring him across to the Mater Hospital but they were afraid to transport him by car.

I got on well with the prison authorities at the time and they told me they were going to make a basketball court in the exercise yard. They asked me to paint a circle in the middle of the yard. I just had to make sure there was enough space for a court. They wanted this big huge circle – with a massive letter H in the middle.

I did what they asked and thought nothing more of it. Me and another fella painted the circle in white. We put this nail into the ground and got this long string. We went around with it. Then we painted the H. The yard itself was covered in tarmacadam. I remember standing there saying this is going to make a great basketball court.

It must have been around tea-time when I heard this helicopter flying overhead. Minutes earlier everyone was told they were going to be locked up. But I went down into the kaput where I used to chat with the wardens.

I knew most of them personally. At the time, MacStioffan was completely isolated. When I heard the noise, I knew exactly what the circle was for. I told the wardens I would be killed for helping them.

But I had the last laugh. In October 1972, the IRA hijacked a helicopter and landed in the same place. Three of the chiefs, including a fella called Kevin Mallon, escaped. Mallon was the main guy at the time. He was in charge of the Provo's border units. The Provos were out in the exercise yard when this helicopter landed much to the astonishment of the prison guards. I think some of them thought it was the Minister for Justice flying in. I would later ask them if they saluted the helicopter when it landed. The boys already knew the helicopter was coming for them.

While the screws were standing to attention, the boys were jumping onto the helicopter, and it was a case of up, up and away.

They were gone before anyone realised what was happening. I remember jeering the prison officers that night. I gave one particular fella some stick.

I didn't see the helicopter land because I was in a different part of the prison but the three of them escaped. I don't know where they went but when we watched the news that night, RTE said the gardaí had set up roadblocks all over the place. We were breaking our bollocks laughing. What's the point in having a roadblock when they are gone in a helicopter?

I maintained my connections with the Provos long after I was released from the Joy. Guns were hard to come by in those days. The Provos often asked me to go off and buy a few guns from criminals who would sell them. I would make my few quid on the deal.

I would mostly buy shotguns. There were very few handguns around Dublin at that time.

I used to meet them in a pub across the road from St. James's Hospital. I would go into the back room and I would bolt the door. We would do our bit of business unknown to the management of the bar.

I thought the Provos were a funny lot. They always pestered me to saw off the barrels of the shotguns. They were paranoid about informers. The two fellas I gave the guns to would never collect a weapon. Instead they would ask me to leave six or seven sawn-offs in a hole on a piece of wasteground they used. They would go mad for walkie-talkies as well. I used to rob these from building sites for them. I never did them favours for free. I didn't believe in doing anything for free. I helped the Republican movement for money.

But there was one time when I actually did help them for free. One morning I got a knock at the door. It was a bird. She said some fella wanted to have a talk with me. I looked out the door expecting to be attacked any moment but I could see no one.

'Who the fuck are you?'

'There's a man over there who knows you and he wants to have a chat.'

It was one of the IRA's chiefs. He was standing outside the flat complex. I walked down to him and told him there was no need for him to introduce himself. The guy asked me to go for a walk.

He kept looking around. This guy was paranoid about Special Branch tailing him. We went for a walk down by the canal behind St. Michael's Estate.

'A friend gave your name to me. This friend of mine said you are very dependable. You know who I represent?'

'How do I know you are not doing this for yourself?'

He never answered the question.

'The reason I need you is because you are a barber. I need you to give a hair cut to a few guys when they finish some work. I will also need five bikes. Five racing bikes.'

He told me to stay at home and have the bikes by the following Tuesday morning. I sorted the bikes out. That was easy. The kids in the flats stole bikes every day of the week from Trinity College.

When Tuesday came, I was sitting out in the grass with my family listening to a record. This car pulled up and these two guys got out. I saw the chief in the back seat. I wandered over to the car and told him I had the bikes he was looking for.

'Get them ready to go in the next hour. One of the boys will show you where.'

The bikes were locked in a friend's shed. He went off for a while and came back with a van. I then took him to the shed.

When we were driving over, he told me to keep my head down. This guy was paranoid about security. I figured there was something big going down.

'This whole place is going to be like a hive with bees trying to get in. These men are probably going to have to stay for two days before they can move to where they are going. We might need you to get them food and things.'

He took me to a house in Crumlin and told me to wait. I waited for about three hours before the five lads were dropped off. I was told to expect a bit of commotion around a certain time. I was sitting in the house, when I saw this van coming up the road. I knew they were after pulling some stroke.

When the five men walked in the door, no one said anything. The only think I could think of saying was, 'Who's first?'

I cut their hair and shaved their beards. Two of them were Northerners. The other three were Dubliners.

I had just finished my work, when the fella who dropped them off returned with a woman with a pram. He walked her to the door of the house, put the money into the pram and left with her immediately.

The five guys had something to eat, and then had a bath. The IRA had held up the CIE works in Inchicore and stolen the payroll. I heard the details on the news that evening. On the second day they went off in different directions. One of them said thanks as they walked out the door.

'Thanks, Bo Bo. If you ever need a favour, you know who to come to. Just go and see the little man with a hat. You know you won't be getting paid for this?'

'I wasn't expecting to get any money.'

I knew the money wasn't for them, otherwise I'd be looking for my full whack.

I never really had any interest in politics, but I believed we needed the IRA, otherwise the Protestants would have walked all over us in the North. I grew to distrust the IRA in later years but I always respected the activists for putting their lives on the line.

chapter twelve

You might think that I forgot about the abuse I suffered in Upton but I didn't. Although I never spoke about it to anyone, the memories of what happened haunted me. I regarded the abuse as the most dramatic thing to ever happen to me. That was until my son Stephen had his accident.

Lobbins had remained a loyal wife to me despite everything. I still don't know what she saw in me. I treated her like dirt in every way possible but she remained true to me even though I wasn't there most of the time. I wasn't there at all.

Our marriage produced six children. Stephen was my third eldest. He was a bright young lad who was always on the run. He was one of these kids who was restless. He always had to be on the move.

One day I was drinking in a pub on Dorset Street with one of my friends when a phone call came. I was a regular there. Everybody knew me. The barman answered the phone and then called me over. It was my daughter Tina.

'Da. Stephen's after falling in the lift. He's hurt.'

'Well, what the fuck are you ringing me for? Bring him over to our Lady's Hospital and get his knee, or his hand sorted out over there. Don't be fucking ringing me here. I'll be home later on and I'll see you then.'

I thought nothing more of the call. A few minutes later one of my neighbours rang. He told me Stephen was critical. He was just five-years-old.

I headed straight to the Richmond Hospital. Lobbins was there. I will never forget the way she looked. She was terrified. She told me Stephen had fallen down a lift shaft. The doors to the lift had opened but there was no lift. He had fallen down six floors. His poor little head had hit an iron girder.

I went numb. I was never a good father to my children. At that moment I wished I could turn back time and smother him in love. All I could think about was Stephen and Lobbins. She was going through pain. And here I was drinking in a bar.

We waited and waited. It was hell. A few hours later, a surgeon came out and told me they were doing everything they possibly could to save Stephen's life, but they didn't think Stephen had a chance. If he did survive, he would be brain damaged. There was nothing they could do.

Lobbins was a great mother. She was a far better person than I ever was. The surgeon told us to go home and get some sleep but we couldn't. It was hypocrisy on my behalf. Weeks often went by where I wouldn't see Stephen. Now when he couldn't talk or see me, I couldn't leave his side.

Stephen didn't regain consciousness. After the second day, we started going home at night. Lobbins spent her time praying that he would recover. Months passed by without any change in his condition.

The turmoil took its toll on Lobbins. It got too much for her and she sank into a depression. She became suicidal. She couldn't cope.

I had to watch her all the time. It came to a situation where I would tie a lace to her leg and tie it around my leg when we went to bed so that if she moved she would wake me. It was hell.

I know I was the real cause of this. I don't mean Stephen's accident but I caused the horrible life she lived. I now realise that she raised those children on her own. She would have been better off without me.

Months of heartache and pressure eventually sent her over the top. She couldn't cope anymore and was admitted to hospital.

I cleaned up my act and just concentrated on Stephen, and his brothers and sisters.

My abusers in the Rosminian Order never broke my spirit but Stephen's accident crushed me. I learned that I had no real friends. My brothers, of course, helped me by giving me money to keep my head above water. My brother Tommy was particularly good. He always made sure I had a few bob in my pocket.

That period of my life is all blurred. I didn't know where I was. Lobbins spent a few weeks in hospital but she was never the same again.

Stephen was unconscious for 14 months but even when he regained consciousness, he couldn't move, talk or even communicate with us.

I remember the day the surgeon came and told us he was awake. I half-expected Stephen to be sitting up in bed. I walked into the room and he looked as if he was asleep. The surgeon knew us all fairly well after such a long time. He sat us down and said that Stephen was never going to recover.

When he fell, his whole skull smashed like an egg. I remember him trying to explain that the cortex fluid around Stephen's brain was lost when his head hit the girder. There was nothing that he or anyone could do. If I had all the money in the world it wouldn't change anything.

This was my child. Here he was lying there. I knew he would never have a life again. This was not right; that was the real tragedy. Nothing good was going to come out of this. And nothing good came out of it.

You might think I am heartless when I say I wish he had died but I'm not. I was a bad father but I loved my children.

But I would have preferred to see Stephen die when he fell. It is okay for people to turn around and say where there's life, there's hope.

There was no hope. I've seen the life but I couldn't find the fucking hope. Stephen's accident stole my heart. I never felt love towards anybody after that. It just took my whole heart away and my whole belief in life.

We moved to Tyrone Place then and I was back in my old district. Stephen's accident drove me more crazy than ever. Although I had never been a responsible father or husband, I continued to refuse my responsibilities. I wouldn't take responsibility for being married. I wouldn't take any kind of responsibility at all. There were weeks when I would go out on a Monday and I wouldn't come home 'till maybe the next Monday. If Lobbins asked me where I was, I'd terrify the woman. I had her living in fear. Anything I said went, and if she didn't do as I told her, she got a beating, which was no way for any woman to live, especially with small children.

You might think the shock of Stephen's accident would have jolted me into reality and that I would want to make up for lost time with my remaining children but it didn't. Responsibility didn't bother me.

I had always whored around with any bird that would go with me, but a lot of the time, I ended up with women by accident. Now I started going out drinking in all the single pubs around Dublin. I'd meet this one and I'd go away with her for a week, I'd come home for two days and then I'd go out and meet someone else.

I just never settled down to marriage. I don't think we should have ever got married really. I blame myself for destroying Lobbins's life, but I wasn't ready for marriage. When I got the opportunity for sex I just ran wild.

If Lobbins hadn't been pregnant for me, someone else would have come along and got pregnant. Nobody sat down and talked to us and said, 'Do you realise what you're getting yourself into, do you realise the responsibility that lies ahead of you? You'll have a family, you'll have to provide for your family, put something away for a rainy day.'

It was like being in Upton again; there was no one there; there was no one you could talk to. I've often asked myself what the hell was wrong with me. I had a beautiful looking girl. The girl I married was a gorgeous looking girl, a lovely girl. I just don't know what happened. Even to the present day I try to sit down and I don't know what happened. I know who is to blame. I know I was to blame, but don't ask me how it all happened.

I ended up in prison for assaulting a garda shortly after Stephen regained consciousness. I attacked this guy for nothing. I was ready to explode with anger over Stephen. I blamed myself for what happened. If I had been a better father would the accident have happened at all? Who knows?

The Department of Justice released me every two weeks to visit my son in hospital. I was now a different man. I spent my time in prison really asking myself where I was going.

I finally came to the conclusion that I wasn't in love with Lobbins although I loved her like a friend. But I also managed to convince myself that there was no love there for the kids.

I think I wanted to leave them because I believed they would be better off; I convinced myself they would be better off. I know they really needed a father who didn't shirk his responsibilities and who would protect them. Instead I started to make plans to abandon them in my mind. Anyone who has been part of a marriage break-up will know the first thing you do is make the break mentally. The physical break-up is usually no problem.

Thinking of Stephen drove me into extreme depression and desperation. I wanted to blame everyone. I ended up being put into a padded cell a couple of times over lashing out at screws. My hatred of authority never left me. If anyone opened their mouth, I'd lash them out of it. Sometimes I was beaten up by other prisoners; they gave back as good as they got.

When I got out of prison I decided I was going to leave Lobbins but when it came to my release I couldn't go through with it. I didn't deserve her and she certainly didn't deserve the life I gave her. She didn't do anything wrong on me; she never went out with anyone behind my back. She wasn't that type of girl.

The only people she ever mixed with were her family. It was all down to me. I was violent and dangerous. I wasn't happy unless I was fighting.

I continued to treat my home like a hotel. I invited people to live with me. I made great money and I lived like a lord. There was nothing that my friends and I needed. I was well-dressed, well-fed, and always had money in my pockets. The thing I never realised was that my wife and kids didn't. I'd give her a few bob just to keep her happy, but I kept the real money for myself. I'd go off with some bird and spend the whole lot on her. I spent all my money on people who didn't matter; people who didn't mean anything. The people who did mean something to me, I didn't give them anything.

I think Stephen's accident haunted me. I could not forget the way he looked. He was by this stage a ward of court. Dublin Corporation paid out hundreds of thousands in compensation for what happened so we decided to put the money in a trust to cover his medical bills.

I used to visit Stephen in hospital the whole time but I could never get used to him just lying there. That kind of thing hits you like a cannon ball. It's the only way I can describe it. Lobbins did everything to save our marriage. She asked me to move home to start over. When we moved everything was fine for a while. I was earning good money from crime. I actually started to save a few pounds. I stopped leaving the house for long periods. I started to take pride in my home.

My plan was to get enough money to buy a nice house and move out of the city. For the first time, I decided I was going to do something with my life and be a proper husband.

My good behaviour rubbed off on my children. They were more confident and started making friends.

Life has always given me surprises. Just when I thought I was turning into a normal husband, my daughter Tina started palling around with a girl that lived down on Till Cannel Road. She was 15-years-old and her name was Eileen Murphy, but everyone called her Lila.

I knew the moment she came into the house that I was going to end up living with her.

My marriage was long over when Lila arrived on the scene. To be honest, Lobbins should never have married me. I was never a good husband to her or a good father. It breaks my heart to say my children would have been better off without me. They deserved so much more than I gave them. I now wish that some cop or gangster had put a bullet through my head and spared them the life I gave them. I was an animal.

I don't think I will ever forgive myself for what I did to them. If I am honest, I have to admit that I ill-treated them all. No, I didn't just ill-treat them; I destroyed their lives.

I beat them viciously and left them all mentally and physically scarred. I tortured them.

My marriage to Lobbins produced six children – four boys and two girls. I named my daughters Tina and Linda. The boys were Stephen, Maurice, Patrick and Martin. I physically abused every one of them.

I know that Maurice tried to commit suicide on more than one occasion for what I had done to him. I would beat him to within an inch of his life if he annoyed me. I attacked the girls. I treated them like dirt. May God forgive me for what I did to them.

I destroyed them. I became their worst nightmare. I was a bastard.

Lobbins lived in fear of her life. I battered her and mutilated her. Our home was hell on earth. I was psychotic. I used to strike her for nothing. If I came home and my dinner wasn't ready, I would beat her up with a frying pan.

I once poured boiling oil over her face. She still bears the scars of our relationship. I broke her jaw in one fight. I used to work out by lifting weights then attack my wife. That's the sort of man I was.

She spent most of her life in homes for battered wives with the children. I look back on those days in horror. I don't know what sort of man I was. I still can't understand why I did what I did. I had no compassion or kindness.

All I wanted to do was beat my wife and fuck other women. I looked on my children as obstacles to having a good time. I brought women home and got off with them in front of my children when Lobbins was out. I would threaten to kill Lobbins if they told her what I was up to. The girls would sit on the couch crying their eyes out as I made out with some slut.

Lobbins had no choice but to stay with me. She believed I would actually kill her. I threatened to murder her if she left. At one stage, she had two permanent black eyes. The girls used to tell their friends that she walked into doors but everyone knew what I was like. And no one would dare go to the gardaí. I would have burned their house down if they said a word.

I beat Lobbins black and blue if she looked at me the wrong way. There were moments when she believed I would actually kill her. I am ashamed of what I did but I was a violent husband and a child beater. Lobbins was forced to take them to hospital several times after I attacked them. The doctors never said anything. They just treated them for the injuries I inflicted. There is no point in me lying. The truth is the truth.

When I met Lila she was just a schoolgirl. There was something about her that drove me wild. She had this innocent look about her. When I saw her I wanted her.

She had moved into our home to help Lobbins look after Stephen and the children. In the beginning, she helped out with the washing and cleaning. I used to give her a few quid to keep an eye on things rather than do any work myself.

Stephen was handicapped. He was a full-time job for Lobbins. Although Lila was supposed to help Lobbins with the cleaning, she ended up being my mistress.

You could say I was sick in the head. I was. Lila was a bit of a young tearaway and I liked that. She was afraid of no one and did whatever she liked.

She would throw me looks that would make my heart jump. I thought she was the greatest bird that ever walked the face of the earth.

When I say that I knew the moment I saw her that we were going to end up with each other, I'm deadly serious. There was this thing between us. I have never been able to explain what it is but it was always there.

I knew I could trust her. She used to look out for me. If the police came looking for me, she would run straight up the stairs to tip me off and I'd be gone out the window.

The moment she started giving me the eye, there was no question of us staying away from each other. When Lobbins would leave the house, I would jump on Lila.

I couldn't keep my hands off her. She made me feel alive. I have to say that I used to feel a bit strange when I would see her palling around with my daughter, Tina, but I got over that.

I didn't care what happened to my family. I only thought about myself. The fact that I had six children including one that was handicapped didn't bother me. That was all the more reason to go. So I walked out on Lobbins when she needed me the most.

When Stephen was hurt I let both him and his mother down. Not only did I walk out on her but I left her with a family and a disabled child. Running away with a teenage girl young enough to be my daughter just rubbed salt into the wounds.

I still remember the day I left home and ran away. Lobbins already knew about Lila but wouldn't believe what she was told because she didn't think that even I could sink that low. When she found out, she went to pieces. Her whole world collapsed but I didn't give a fuck. I was now with a bird half my age and that was all that mattered to me.

Lobbins knew I had been with other women but I think she was more upset for Lila. She knew Lila had her own problems. I think Lobbins was more upset because she saw Lila throwing her life away. She knew what future lay ahead for Lila.

None of that mattered. When I decided to take Lila as my full-time partner, I forced Lobbins to look after the children and help support us. I gave her forms to sign that helped me get a new council house. I made her pretend that I was caring for the children and needed a new house.

I had beaten and abused Lobbins her whole life. Now I was forcing her to watch another young girl go through the same thing. I know this now but such thoughts didn't cross my mind, not even for a second, back in those days.

But I have to say that just about everyone hated my guts for running away with Lila. I discovered that just about everyone in the underworld thought I was a bastard. Gangsters are funny like that. They have no problem shooting people dead and selling drugs but they will look down their noses at you if you leave your wife.

When they heard that I had moved into a flat with Lila, some of them started ignoring me. I didn't give a fuck. I was getting what I wanted.

chapter thirteen

The crime scene changed in the 1980s when drugs hit the streets of Dublin. Drugs were always available to certain people but they didn't get a foothold in the city. All that changed in 1980 when Larry Dunne started importing heroin, which he sold to children in the flats.

Larry Dunne changed the face of the Irish crime scene. You could say the arrival of heroin signalled a new era.

When I was a boy growing up in the tenements all those years ago, there were no junkies. The people who lived in the flats didn't live in constant fear of standing on a syringe. The young girls and boys didn't sell their bodies to feed an addiction.

When I say drugs destroyed the fabric of the inner city, I mean it wiped out whole families.

Children who grew up in places like Fatima Mansions and St. Theresa's Gardens didn't stand a chance. The dealers turned them into zombies.

Until that time I had only robbed banks, factories and houses. I wasn't into fraud or prostitution. I provided muscle to different gangs if they required it but that was all.

If I am going to be honest I have to admit I got deeply involved in the heroin trade with a fella called Eddie Johnson, a smack dealer from Fatima Mansions who oversaw a distribution operation for Larry Dunne and his brother Mickey, the Dazzler. It's a period of my life that I'd rather forget about but I honestly didn't know what heroin did to people. I suppose I didn't want to know because Johnson and the two Dunne brothers paid me huge money to protect them.

When I say Larry Dunne was the Mr. Big of the Dublin underworld; that is an understatement. He was ruthless. He started out as a robber but moved into drug dealing. He became the Don Corleone of the Dublin underworld.

Every robber in the city wanted to do business with Larry Dunne. He was Ireland's first drug baron. The word on the street was that Americans, Africans, Spanish and Dutch drug traffickers supplied him. Dunne used to import heroin from places like

Pakistan through Amsterdam. Most Dubliners couldn't show you where Pakistan was on a map. This was big time crime. The Dunnes were a Mafia. The mention of Larry Dunne's name was enough to strike the fear of God into anyone. He was the Pablo Escobar of Ireland.

At the time, I was hanging around with this criminal from London. His name was Tony. He was a dangerous bastard. Tony had spent most of his life behind bars for blagging and extortion. I knew he had worked with some heavy crews from London's East End.

I would describe him as an enforcer. He was the type of man who would exact revenge on someone no matter how long it took him. He took no shit from anyone. He'd also kick the crap out of you for a few quid.

I met him when he moved to Dublin. We used to go for a few pints. I liked him from the moment I met him because he could hold his drink, and didn't give a fuck. He was a criminal who had loads of money and bottle. You had to respect a guy like that.

I remember we were in a pub on Parnell Street drinking one day. I wanted to know where he was getting all the cash from so I pretended to be broke.

I said, 'Fuck it, I'm going down to the pawnshop. I have two rings. I should get around £40 for these rings. I need a few quid.'

'Don't do that, Bo Bo. I have a couple of mates around the corner. I'll get you a job if you want.'

'What do you mean a job?'

'A job. Don't worry, there will be nice money in it. Big money if you are up for it.'

We left the pub a few minutes later and he brought me to these two guys that were selling drugs for Larry Dunne's gang. Like everyone else, I knew Larry. I knew him and Mickey were major drug dealers.

I had smoked a bit of hash, but as far as drugs were concerned, I didn't know anything else.

Tony spoke to these two guys on his own. He arranged a meeting for the next day with Larry Dunne, his brother Mickey and this guy called Eddie Johnson. I couldn't believe my luck. I was now joining the most dangerous gang in Ireland. I was over the moon.

I can't recall where I met them but I do remember that I didn't recognise Larry and Mickey when they arrived for the meeting the next day, they was so well-dressed. They were dressed up to the nines.

Larry was the same as always. I knew Larry from prison and I had known his father, Bronco.

We used to go down to Glendalough – me and him in the summer time. When people were going for walks, the birds would leave their handbags behind in the car. So we had a thing like a biro. It would break the glass. This thing would shoot out like a bullet, and then we would open the door and lift the bags.

You would only need to make a couple of touches a day and you would walk away with a couple of hundred quid each.

I actually knew the whole family, right the way down to the girls. I heard people saying that Larry Dunne was dirt. I would have a fight with them over that. He had this way about him. He didn't say more than he had to. Larry was making so much money at the time that he thought he was above everyone else, which in fairness to him was true.

Eddie Johnson was also there. Johnson lived in Fatima Mansions. He was an addict who had a few minor convictions for drugs. He ran a dry cleaning business in Harold's Cross and he had access to a lock-up garage on Meath Street.

Larry and Mickey didn't want to talk in front of me. Larry was facing charges at the time and he was paranoid. He knew the cops had recruited a spy in the camp. He certainly didn't trust me.

Eddie Johnson took Tony into a little room for a more private talk with the Dunnes. He came out a few minutes later and patted me on the shoulder and asked me to step outside.

'I can get you £1000 a week.'

'For what?'

'Just to stand there.'

Johnson wanted me to protect the lock-up on Meath Street. They were offering to pay me £1000 to stand outside and watch for the cops or anyone else. The garage was the holding point for the heroin they were selling into St. Theresa's Gardens and the south inner city.

I jumped at the chance. A grand a week for standing around looking at birds walking by sounded great to me.

I started guarding the place the next day. No one came near the place. I knew every criminal in the south inner city. They knew how violent I was. If they came near the lock-up they would have to deal with me. Few would dare to have a go.

I saw the heroin trade work from the inside out. Johnson smuggled small amounts of smack into the garage where it would be cut up.

This fella used to arrive with a bag of powder. This was his golden brown. They treated it like gold. They would all sit around a table in the lock-up staring at the heroin. The weigher, as I used to call him, would wipe down the table, then place a small weighing scales in the centre. He would have loads of plastic bags. This guy would put a spoon into the powder and weigh it. He would then cut the heroin into quarters and half ounces. He put glucose into it before he mixed it.

The couriers would then arrive, collect the deals and go off again. This happened every day.

I used to go into the garage in the morning, and I would leave at around 4.30 p.m. when business would finish. I just stood there to make sure that no one robbed anything.

Once the heroin was dispatched, the guy who cut the deal would inject himself. He was a junkie. I often left him fast asleep with a needle in his arm inside that garage.

On the way home I would see the addicts congregating in gangs around Meath Street. They would pay anything for the smack: handbags, jewellery and even their bodies. I don't know how many young girls offered me blow jobs and sex to score them an ounce. They were pathetic. I wouldn't go near them because they looked horrible.

The money the two Dunnes and Johnson turned over had to be seen to be believed. They had boxes full of gold bracelets and diamond rings – anything you could want. They left thousands of pounds lying around the whole time.

I remember trying to steal about £15,000 I found hidden in a biscuit-tin, but one of the gang saw me taking the money to my car. I was never one to miss an opportunity. I had seen someone hiding the money and then get strung out.

They had so much money I didn't think they would even notice it had gone missing. I was actually out the door with the money when someone shouted, 'What are you doing with that?'

'With what?'

'That fucking tin, all the money is in that tin.'

'What do you pay me for? I look after the money. There's a load of scumbags in there. No one will touch my fucking car. Did you think I was robbing the cash?'

I was indeed robbing the money but they didn't know what to think. If they had pushed the issue I would have beaten them to a pulp. Even Larry Dunne wouldn't have wanted a fight with me.

I provided security to the two Dunnes and Johnson for about two months but I never saw kids arriving at the door; it was all old-time junkies. They would come in three or four times a day.

The money I earned allowed me to set up home with Lila. I rented a house in Blanchardstown, where I was doing a bit of business on the side. I used to say to myself, 'God bless the drugs trade.'

I did my own bit of business around Dublin. I set up my own heroin ring, which also made me money. They were happy days. I never had it so good. One morning, I was in the house when the door came crashing in. It was the drugs squad. The detectives were armed.

I was asleep in bed when they stormed the room. One guy held me down while another asked me for the keys of my car.

I had been raided by the gardaí scores of times but this time was different. They were more aggressive and they genuinely seemed to hate me. They made a point of pushing me around.

One of them even called me a fucking scumbag. I had spent my life on the wrong side of the law but this was over the top.

'Have you got a problem?'

'Yeah I do. You're a smack dealer.'

'I'm not selling drugs.'

'Cop on, Bo Bo. You are the muscle man for Larry and Mickey Dunne and Johnson. You might as well be selling the drugs yourself.'

The detectives held me against the wall for about 30 minutes before they let me sit down. They didn't know I was dealing on the side.

They had found nothing. I knew the sergeant in charge of the raid and asked him what their problem was. I hadn't cut up rough. He asked me to come outside to where no one was listening.

'You were always a fucking thief, Bo Bo. What are you doing working with the Dunnes and Johnson?'

'What?'

'You rob houses. No one gets killed. You know what the Dunnes and Johnson are doing to the kids. They are all junkies. Have you walked into Fatima Mansions and seen what's going on? If we don't get you, the Provos will. This is getting bad, Bo Bo.'

'All I am doing is stopping your man from getting robbed. Isn't that better than jumping over a counter with a fucking shotgun or breaking into people's houses?'

'I'd prefer to see you breaking into houses. Or going over counters with shotguns.'

I didn't know what to do. I told him to fuck off. I thought he was jealous but the Rosser started me thinking.

I started looking at the junkies. I saw people I had known all my life looking like shit. I never really thought about drug dealing or about what I was doing.

The scene got much heavier. The Rosser was right when he said the IRA was going to start targeting the pushers. They did.

The people of the inner city set up a group called the Concerned Parents Against Drugs. They evicted the dealers from the flats and threatened the pushers. Everyone knew the IRA was backing them up.

I was providing security at the lock-up. If the Provos came to murder Johnson, I would be the one man standing in their way.

You might say it would have been better if I was killed but I genuinely didn't realise what was happening. The only person I saw sticking a needle in his arm was the weigher.

I suppose I never saw the addicts as real people or looked at the effects the drug had on their parents and home life.

I am allergic to needles. I faint when I get an injection. I could never understand why someone would want to stick a needle into their arm.

I couldn't give up the job because the money was too good. I continued to provide muscle at the door of the lock-up. It was such an easy job and I was earning a fortune. I took the view that I would deal with trouble if and when it arrived.

I had been involved in crime my whole life. I can honestly say that I was never frightened. I never felt I was getting too deep into something. I stopped doing armed robberies because I was afraid that I would kill someone, I didn't stop because I was afraid of the gardaí or anyone else.

When I was involved with Johnson and the Dunne brothers I felt different. The whole business was heavy. The newspapers were full of stories about Larry Dunne. The whole country knew about his family.

One day a detective walked up to me outside the garage and told me to get out of the area. He was trying to give me a hint but I told him to fuck off.

The place was raided later that day. I have to admit that I didn't see them coming. One guy just walked up to me, pushed me against the wall and had me handcuffed before I knew what was going on.

I told him I was carrying nothing but he didn't care. He gave me a clatter. I told him I was going to rape him and his mother which sent him into a rage. He went for me but I sidestepped him and ducked underneath him. The other coppers then dragged me into a squad car and off to Kevin Street garda station where they strip-searched me. They got a doctor who searched my bum. I went mad. I asked for a garda that I knew.

'What the fuck is going on here?'

'We know you are not into this but you are working for the two Dunnes and Johnson.'

This was definitely getting too heavy for me. When the police tell doctors to start searching your insides, it's time to call it a day.

I never had a conscience. I never really cared about anyone else. I didn't gave a shit about who I hurt. When I worked for Johnson and the two Dunnes I turned a blind eye to the junkies. Imagine earning £1000 a week in 1981. I don't mind saying this but I found it difficult to complain about anything. I had a young bird on my arm and all the money in the world.

I had already made up my mind to get out of the heroin trade when one of my friends came to me about his daughter.

I knew this guy well. He was a robber and had served time with me. He asked me for a meeting, so I met him in The Clock pub on Thomas Street. He looked as if he had been crying. I thought he had cancer or something. I asked him what was wrong with him.

'My daughter is on heroin.'

'So what?'

'What do you mean so what? My daughter is taking fucking heroin.'

'So what? What's she taking – tablets?'

'She's taking fucking heroin! She's injecting herself!'

The guy went to pieces in front of everyone. I knew the girl since she was a baby. She was a nice kid. She was good looking which made my mate afraid.

'They are going to put her on the game Bo Bo. Can you do anything?'

'On the fucking game? Just tell her to stop using the stuff.'

I think that was the first time I realised that heroin addicts couldn't stop taking drugs. The story screwed me up.

I didn't need anyone to tell me I would be in trouble if I just walked away. You don't resign from a criminal gang. Men who leave gangs always quit for a reason, which brings them into conflict with their former mates. If you know too much about a gang you are a risk because you can talk to the police. No one turns over a new leaf. If one guy leaves, it's normally to set up a rival gang.

I decided the best way out was to shut Johnson down. And I knew there was only one way to do that.

I couldn't murder him because I would have spent the rest of my life running from Larry and Mickey Dunne. I did something I swore I would never do. I became a garda informer.

In October 1982 Johnson mentioned that he had a big shipment arriving. The heroin was going to his dry cleaning firm in Harold's Cross; he didn't want the haul to go anywhere near the lock-up in Meath Street because it was getting too hot there. The cops sat outside morning, noon and night.

Johnson wanted me to provide security for the shipment while it was being delivered. If I saw anything strange, I was to let him know. He told me the shipment was going to be divided between Mickey and Larry Dunne. He wanted everything to run smoothly.

The drugs were delivered on 11 November by one of the mules. When the courier made the drop, the drugs were moved straight to Harold's Cross. I followed the guy who carried the smack to make sure no one was watching or following. When I was sure the coast was clear, I walked in the door where I saw Johnson putting the heroin into a cistern behind a wall. This was his hiding place. When he was finished, I said goodbye and headed off. I left Johnson there with the drugs.

There were no mobile telephones in those days so I went to the nearest phone box I could find and called the drugs squad. I asked for a detective I knew.

'Do you know who this is?'

'Yes.'

'You probably won't believe me but do you know Eddie Johnson?'

'Yes.'

'Do you know where his dry cleaners is?'

'Yes.'

'There is over £2 million worth of heroin in the central heating system around the walls.'

'Are you sure Bo Bo?'

'I wouldn't tell you otherwise. You'd want to be moving on this. And I'll tell you who you'll catch there as well. You will catch Larry Dunne and Mickey Dunne because they are due over. Now fuck off.'

The drugs squad seized heroin worth £400,000 in the dry cleaners. It was a massive capture. I think it was the biggest of its kind. I think they put the place under surveillance. The two Dunnes never showed but the gardaí got the drugs. This was my way of making up for all the wrong I had done.

About a week later, I was walking along Francis Street when I saw the copper I had tipped off. He was driving along. He pulled in down the road, stepped out of the car and walked up to meet me. There were two guys with him watching out for trouble. I spoke before he got a chance to open his mouth.

'It was a one-off. You won't be hearing from me again, no matter what's going down.'

I kept on walking. I never heard from him again.

Johnson knew I had grassed him out though no one would believe him. He was convicted a year later. He got 12 years. His lawyers begged the court to treat him leniently because he was an addict and had a family. The judge was having none of it.

He ended up selling all his vans and his dry cleaner business as well. He went bust.

The raid was the beginning of the end for Larry Dunne. His operation fell to pieces afterwards.

I think Dunne always suspected me of grassing on Johnson but he never said anything. He had his own problems. He didn't want to start a row with me because I would have murdered him. You can't call a man a grass and expect to get away with it. The Dazzler also went down.

In the months that followed, the gardaí persecuted me. They didn't leave me alone for about four years until I had lost every penny. I suppose I didn't deserve any better.

I have to say that most of the old time gangsters didn't know much about drugs. I didn't know anything. I used to say, 'What's fucking wrong with selling drugs?' When you are actually involved in shipping drugs and you are getting nice money there is no problem.

I made easy money with the two Dunnes. I never made such easy money. The money roped you in.

When I joined Johnson I didn't know what heroin even looked like. I was street wise and I was a thief but I was still very innocent in regards to drugs. When I saw what was actually going on, I got out. When I saw kids who were starting to die, I took action.

I thought grassing on Eddie Johnson was the best way out of it. Do I regret making the phone call to the drugs squad? The answer to that question is both yes and no. I regret co-operating with the gardaí but I regret my time with Larry and Mickey Dunne even more.

chapter fourteen

Ratting out the two Dunnes and Johnson didn't turn me into a law-abiding citizen. I went back to robbing immediately to earn a living. Johnson told just about anyone who would listen to him that I was a rat but no one would believe him.

Though I have to admit that a few crews gave me the cold shoulder; they were afraid the cops had recruited me as an informer. Anyone who really knew me didn't believe a word but a few of them were not willing to take the risk. Criminals will do anything to save their own skins; it's an occupational hazard.

I was lucky that not one of the old school believed Johnson. They hated drugs. I think some of these guys wouldn't have even cared if I confessed to ratting.

After my encounter with heroin, I decided to stick to what I knew best. I put the feelers out that I was looking for straight work; that is robbing factories and houses.

The biggest crew operating at the time was the Hole in the Wall gang. A young guy nicknamed Warehouse John headed the outfit but I knew him as young John Gilligan.

You might recall that I robbed shops in the north inner city with his father, John, when I was just a boy. Young John was just 18-years-old when I last met him. At that time, I had moved in with his family after I burned down a shop whose owner had ripped off my mother.

The Rossers were looking for me, so one of my friends took me to Ballyfermot where I met up with old Gilligan. He was good to me. He took me into his home where I lived for about four months. The only thing I remember about the house was that it was full of people.

Young Gilligan was about 18-years-old and worked for Irish Ferries. I didn't think he was even stroking at the time.

When he went into crime, he was a success. He built up a small crew that would rob anything to sell on. The gang became the best hijackers and warehouse robbers in Dublin. They could clear a warehouse in the space of a few hours. When I say he would rob the eyes out of your head I mean just that. He turned over loads of money because he saw money in everything and was willing to take risks. The other thing that made him unique was that he never ripped off the men who worked with him. He always made sure everyone got their fair share. I never found Gilligan to be mean. I never had any problem getting any money off him. He had great principles that way.

I joined forces with the Hole in the Wall gang after one of the gang vouched for me. Gilligan knew me of old and was more than delighted to have me on board.

The gang operated between the industrial estates of Tallaght and Clondalkin. Gilligan himself would scout the industrial estates of west Dublin in stolen vans and trucks, break into warehouses himself and then return with the gang to take everything.

He would sit down and plan out the last detail of every robbery. He would lie in ditches just watching factories. He used to call this 'studying the form.'

He used to come up with ingenious ways to break into factories. I remember lighting bonfires using old timber and pallets against factory walls with him. He would let the fire burn for hours.

Everything was planned like a fucking military operation.

He would return with a truck and a full crew and smash a hole in the wall. The fire would have dried out the bricks and mortar. When the boys would attack it with a sledge-hammer, they would make a big hole within minutes. Gilligan would direct the operation using a walkie-talkie. When he got inside a factory, he didn't leave anything behind. When I say he took everything, I mean everything.

Gilligan didn't just break-in, load up and drive off as fast as possible. He would bring in two lorries and three vans to clean the place out.

I have to admit that I loved working with Gilligan. He was the most sophisticated robber of his time.

I liked him because he wasn't selective about the loot. I remember breaking into a warehouse with him and he even stole a spare tyre from a truck parked in the loading bay. I never had any problems with John. I always respected him. He was a great worker.

I think the gardaí even came to conclude that he was unstoppable. When the cops would foil a robbery, he always had another factory in line.

The older generation of criminals looked on him as a protégée. When he turned 30 years of age, he had great connections to fence stolen goods. He knew doctors, vets, bankers and high flyers in the business world. I never found out how he knew these people but he did.

He stuck to warehouse robberies in the early 1980s but he moved into other crime. By 1983, he was doing mail van and payroll robberies. He made a right few quid out of that.

When I would meet Gilligan on the street, I used to call him a lucky bastard. He was unstoppable. Even when the cops caught him he walked away from the charges.

I remember he was caught red-handed robbing a consignment of Nilfisk vacuums. They actually arrested him with the stolen gear in a warehouse but when the case came to court, he was released on a legal technicality.

Very few people know that Gilligan fenced animal products, tablets and medical gear. He would ask every criminal in Dublin to try to find someone who worked with pharmaceuticals. He even had connections capable of shifting stolen medicines.

Needless to say I soon found someone who worked inside a medical factory in the Bluebell Industrial Estate. I knew this guy very well. I must say I never found it hard to recruit insiders in companies and banks.

You have to remember that everyone was penniless in the 1980s. There were no jobs and people couldn't afford the price of a cup of tea. Money was scarce. Most working-class men with large families jumped at the chance at making a little extra money.

My friend robbed a bag of tablets from a factory where he worked as a security guard. I had put the word out that I was in the game for medicines. This guy arrived at my front door with a Quinnsworth bag filled with tiny white tablets. He said they were worth serious money. I hadn't a clue. They could have been aspirins for all I knew, but I took ten of them, wrapped them in a tissue and headed over to meet Gilligan's right hand man. This guy was called Mick.

Mick was a good friend of mine. He used to visit my home three or four times a week. You could say he was more loyal to me than he was to Gilligan.

Mick took the tablets over to Gilligan's house in Blanchardstown. I hadn't seen him in ages because I had started to do my own thing. If I remember correctly, he was keeping a low profile at the time.

Gilligan took a close look at the tablets. He didn't know what they were but he knew someone who might. He told me to go and see his mate Tommy Coyle in Drogheda.

Coyle was the godfather of Drogheda. He saw himself as some sort of Don Corleone. He was involved in just about every type of scam going. He was a drug runner, a bootlegger and fraudster. Nothing happened along the border without his approval.

The funny thing is that everyone knew he worked for the gardaí and British police but for some reason people still did business with him. If you think I am exaggerating, he was arrested with stolen bonds worth £77 million at Heathrow Airport while catching a flight to Miami.

Coyle told the Brits he was on his way to Florida to buy a racehorse. About two weeks later, the charges were dropped against him. The whole world knew he had set up the seizure for a reward.

In fairness he had a sense of humour. He bought a racehorse the following year and called it £77mill.

When Gilligan told me to talk to him, I looked at him.

'Are you for fucking real? Coyle sets people up for the gardaí.'

'He won't do anything once I'm involved.'

I drove to Drogheda that night with Mick to meet up with Coyle. It was a fucking joke. The gardaí were parked across the road watching his house when we arrived.

Coyle invited the two of us into his sitting room and asked us to take a seat. I handed him the tablets while keeping an eye on the door.

He didn't seem too concerned about the gardaí watching the house. They scared the shit out of me. He took the tablets and we left.

He sent a message to me a week later and paid me a few grand to get more of them. It was happy days for a few weeks anyway.

I started getting more involved with Coyle and Gilligan. I think Gilligan became a bit bored with the Hole in the Wall so he started doing a bit of fraud along with the warehouse robberies. I know he was kiting stolen cheques. Gilligan then started fencing loot robbed by some of the other crews around Dublin.

Gilligan used to ask me to sell this stuff on his behalf. I brought most of the stuff to Cork. I had a mate down there called Charlie. He knew everyone in the underworld and everyone knew him.

Gilligan was unstoppable for about four years. He must have robbed every factory in Ireland at some stage but his luck ran out in late 1989 when he got nicked. He was caught red-handed with stolen goods.

I think he was expecting to get nabbed. He had walked away scot-free from charges a few times on legal technicalities. Gilligan was the type of guy who was clever enough to know that his luck was running out.

When Gilligan was sent away to the maximum-security wing in Portlaoise Prison. I started doing more business with Coyle.

He was without doubt the most untrustworthy villain you could ever meet. That might sound rich coming from the likes of me but I will explain what I mean.

All criminals know they can never trust anyone they work with, but they hope their fellow thieves remain loyal once they are earning money.

Coyle wasn't one of these people. He was more slippery than an eel you would catch in the River Liffey.

He never stopped devising ways of pulling fast ones on people. Stroking was in his nature. And the best strokes he organised were not against innocent victims but other criminal gangs.

Coyle thought these scams were great because he knew the victims could never report the matter to the gardaí.

Let me explain what I mean. I got involved in one scam with Coyle where we stung members of the Ulster Defence Association for £26,000.

Mick had come to me and asked if I wanted to get involved in a scam. I asked if the job would be dangerous, because you don't want some fucking bastard shooting you dead for a few quid.

Mick didn't answer the question but said there would be massive money so I agreed. Things were tight money-wise. I said I would take a chance.

Coyle had managed to get his hands on a small amount of stolen platinum. The bastard came up with a plan to sell the metal to a gang from the UDA in Belfast. He had some contact up there.

The stroke would work like this. Coyle would approach the UDA and say he had three tea chests of platinum.

He would invite the UDA to inspect the gear at some factory in Dublin, where the platinum was being stored. Coyle would tell the UDA that he had a security guard in his pocket, who would allow his gang to steal the platinum, but only when he had a buyer for it.

Only Coyle could come up with this scam. The amazing thing was that Coyle had the whole thing up and running by the time I got involved.

Mick had found an abandoned warehouse in Tallaght. He had cleaned the place up and put new locks on the doors. All he wanted me to do was make it look like a proper warehouse.

It seemed straightforward to me. I went off and got security guard uniforms from a friend of mine. I even got two German Shepherd dogs. Coyle made arrangements to bring the loyalists down from Belfast.

When I say Coyle was a slippery eel, he was the type of fella who would sell sand to Arabs. He enjoyed the stroke more than the money he earned.

On the day before the UDA were due to arrive, he went off and bought a few bars of platinum. It came in little balls. Coyle had one of his fence friends melt the metal into small cubes.

He sent one or two of the platinum cubes to Belfast as a good will gesture. He knew the UDA would go off and have the samples analysed to see how pure it was.

Coyle was a sly bastard if ever there was one. He knew the minute the UDA had the platinum tested, they would come straight back to him. And that's exactly what happened.

When the Loyalists made contact, Coyle told them he was in danger of losing the shipment. You see, fraud of this kind is all about building up the victim's confidence.

I remember him falling around the place laughing when he sent word to the UDA saying it was essential that he cut the deal fast. The UDA took the bait but they were afraid. They knew their necks were on the line if anything went wrong.

As a goodwill gesture, Coyle offered to bring the loyalists to the factory where they could examine the metal for themselves.

This is where he introduced the trick. He told them if they were interested, they would have to bring a deposit.

The UDA demanded another sample but Coyle refused. He said he couldn't get another sample because the one he had given them already weighed a pound and was worth around £1,600. This made perfect sense to the UDA and they accepted his story.

Coyle didn't mind sacrificing the cash for the big sting. The UDA agreed to send a delegation to Dublin to oversee the deal.

And this is where I came in. When they arrived, I pretended to be Coyle's insider in the precious metals factory. I got my friends to dress up as security guards and walk around with the dogs. They looked the part.

Coyle brought the two UDA men to Dublin where they met me. I took them out to the warehouse in my car.

When I arrived at the gates, I called out to my friend who was dressed as a security guard. I pretended to be a security manager and ordered him to let me into the factory. I actually told him I had some important paperwork to do. They even questioned me about my business before letting me through.

I took the UDA men through the front door and into an office where we had left four crates. Coyle had bought more platinum, which he placed in small boxes in the first tea chest.

The UDA guys examined the little bars of metal and agreed to hand over a deposit of £6,000. We then drove to Castleblaney in Co. Monaghan where they had a guy waiting with the cash. He handed me the bag.

There is always a danger that something will go seriously wrong with this type of fraud. As a precaution, I carried a handgun. As far as I was concerned, loyalists were more than capable of killing me.

Once the deposit was paid, I was supposed to deliver the rest of the platinum to Belfast. This is where the stroke became really dangerous.

Coyle told the UDA I would personally deliver the metal to Belfast once I got the money. But when I got the first deposit, I said I was not leaving the goods until I got full payment. I was, after all, risking my career in the factory.

The UDA agreed but then Coyle changed the location of the drop to the Coachman's Inn near Dublin airport. I pretended to be annoyed with this. I left with the £6,000 and returned to Dublin.

Coyle had told the UDA we would hand over the platinum at the Coachman's Inn beside Dublin Airport. When I turned up, three men from the UDA met me. They were covered from head to toe in tattoos of the Union Jack. I was on my own.

When they stepped out of the car, I said there was a hitch and I told him to ring Coyle. He told them he wanted the money handed over first. He promised to deliver the platinum in five minutes.

The UDA guys were convinced we were legitimate so they handed over another £20,000 to keep us sweet. Once the money was paid, we vanished. One of them sent a message to Coyle afterwards telling him that he was a dead man but he didn't care.

While Gilligan was serving his time in Portlaoise Prison, no one went to visit him. There is an unwritten code of conduct among thieves. We don't visit each other in prison but we look after each other when we are released and do favours when asked.

When Gilligan was released, he got into a lot of trouble. There were a few guys threatening him and trying to bully him. He sent word to me that he needed help.

I arranged to go over to his place in Blanchardstown to sort out his problem. Gilligan was not into violence. I remember him being too afraid to face this guy down. He actually stood at the back of a van and pointed this guy out to us. We knew he was too afraid to be seen but we pretended we didn't want him to come with us so nobody could pin it on him. But we all knew he was scared.

I brought my two guys with me and we caught this fella who was threatening Gilligan. We gave him a good beating. I told him that if he stepped out of line again, then that would be the end of him.

Gilligan always had money. He took me out drinking that night. We met up in Chapelizod and got jarred in the Mullingar House. After a few pints, he asked me into the toilets where he gave me a block of money and the keys to a Fiat Regata. I didn't have a car at the time. Gilligan was good like that.

I did a few other things for Gilligan back in those days. I remember one stroke the two of us pulled shortly after he was freed.

Gilligan was one of these guys who never stopped looking out for opportunities to fleece someone. When he was on his travels, he noticed this guy selling veterinary products at a cattle mart in Cork. This guy drove a Mercedes – a big white one. I think he was selling animal products to the farmers.

Gilligan sent for me and told me that if we stole this man's load, we could earn £20,000. We ended up following this man from mart to mart in Cork to see where he lived. To make sure he actually lived there, we watched him for the whole day.

We stole everything from the sheds around his home and moved it straight to Drogheda. Gilligan had a storage place there. We made a killing on that job. He sold the whole load to some vet.

But Gilligan soon got back to his old ways. He got involved in every sort of crime. He started fleecing everyone around him.

I knew a lot of builders and I used to do a bit of security work. Gilligan asked me to arrange for some mates of mine who worked as security men to take their tea breaks at certain times. When they went off to the shop, he would rob all the building machinery.

I would give small time security guards £35 and they would let us steal the JCBs and the dumpers. Gilligan would have them sold before they even left the site.

I admired him for his cunning but he was dealing with the police all the time. People may find that hard to believe but everyone knew he was an informer. When he walked away from serious charges, the gardaí always made some big seizure; that was the trade off.

Gilligan went on to become Ireland's biggest drugs baron. The strange thing is that he became a multimillionaire overnight.

I remember when he got involved in the drugs business. I only knew Gilligan as a really good thief but the word on the street was that he was importing serious amounts of drugs.

I knew he was doing business with John Traynor, a fraudster from the southside. He was a known informer. I heard the two of them were importing huge shipments of cigarettes and cannabis.

I knew about the contraband cigarettes. Gilligan's right-hand man Mick used to drop four cartons, which contained ten packets, over to my house every Friday. He said they were his – but I knew they belonged to Gilligan. The smokes would only be in my gaff for ten minutes and I would make £125 profit by having a few people ready to buy them. If I could make that amount of money in ten minutes, Gilligan was raking it in.

When I heard that he was involved in drugs I couldn't believe it. I suppose I was fucking thick in my own way.

I should have known. It all happened so fast. He lost touch with the robbers. The next thing I heard was that he had built this mansion near Enfield in Kildare for his wife. Then I heard he was flying around the world with Brian Meehan and Paul Ward. Meehan was a stupid little prick from Crumlin who wanted to be the next Martin Cahill. Ward was just a junkie but he was okay.

I knew them all. I remember asking Paul Ward what they were doing and he said it was only hash.

I have to admit I smoked it myself – but I didn't want to get involved. Word spreads quickly when people are making serious money.

When I found out that Gilligan and Ward were now into this big time, I didn't know what to think. To be honest I didn't believe they could be millionaires. But I soon learned how wrong I was.

I remember Ward owed me a few favours so I got a mobile number for him and rang to see if I could get a few quid.

He sent this bird to see me. I didn't know this bird so I told her that I had to see him. I wasn't going to have a chat with some tart.

I told her I would be in a certain pub at 7.30 p.m. in the city centre. He arrived on time.

Ward came in all dressed up. He ordered a round of drinks and sat down. I came straight to the point and asked him for some money.

I said that I wanted a car to do some work down the country.

'£2,000 will do me for the car and the insurance. I will give you a cut from every job.'

'I'll be back in an hour Bo Bo.'

'Are you going to fuck off and let me down?'

'I'll be back in an hour Bo Bo.'

True to his word, he came back and handed me a bag. He just said, 'Here you go,' and he walked out again.

I walked into the toilet and nearly dropped dead when I opened the bag. It was full of money. When I got home, I counted £5,500. And they didn't want it back.

I went back looking for money a few times. They would give me a couple of grand every six months. I always asked did they want the money back but they said no. They offered me work loads of times but I said no. I could see where they were going to end up. Brian Meehan was driving brand new jeeps and Gilligan was travelling around like Donald Trump. He even had a young bird behind Geraldine's back. He was the man. I have to admit I was tempted but I said no.

chapter fifteen

Most old school gangsters like Gilligan got involved in drug dealing because the money was huge. The newspapers say Gilligan made about £50 million but I reckon he made more. I was told the money was buried in a lorry container hidden underground. You might laugh at this but it makes perfect sense. If you knew John Gilligan like I do you'd know this is exactly what he'd do.

While you may think that criminals become less likely to use violence when they are making serious money, this could not be further from the truth. Drug dealing made the Dublin underworld more dangerous.

Let me tell you a story about Johnny Reddin, a friend of mine from the old days. Johnny was shot dead while having a drink in The Blue Lion pub on Parnell Street in 1996. A guy walked into the bar and blew his fucking head off.

I had an idea that Johnny was into drugs. But I found it hard to dump him as a friend. If I am hanging around with a guy for my entire life, and he trips or makes a mistake, I am fucked if I am going to hold that against him.

A few weeks before he was shot, I confronted him and asked him out straight if he was shifting dope. He said he was and told me how much money he was making. He was making £10,000 a week and he didn't even handle anything. He had all these little soldiers running around doing his dirty work. I couldn't believe the money he was making. I even considered going back into the heroin game myself.

Johnny got shot dead over ecstasy. Some fella sold him a load of fake tablets and Johnny slit the guy's throat. A friend of the guy retaliated by putting a contract on Johnny. Hey presto, he's dead.

When I was robbing warehouses that type of thing rarely happened. There was some honour among the thieves. But those days are long gone now. There are no robbers left.

When drugs made a big comeback in the early 1990s, the crews got involved in drug dealing because the money was massive and the chances of getting caught were slim. I don't think the gardaí knew, or could bring themselves to believe, how much money was being made.

I know for a fact that anyone who did business with Gilligan made a fortune. He knew that no one would rat him out once he kept his inner circle sweet.

I have to admit I wasn't that shocked when he was implicated in the murder of the journalist from the *Sunday Independent*, Veronica Guerin. When millions of pounds are at stake, criminals are capable of anything.

People like you often ask me why the guys don't stop when they make their first million. I always give the same answer. Criminals sell drugs to make money. They make more money through drug dealing than you can even imagine. When they make their first million, no one wants to know how or where it came from; they only want to know if they can do it again.

Remember what I said. Crime is like a drug. When you rob for the first time, when you make a grand for the first time, when you shoot someone for the first time, it gives you a special feeling. You spend the rest of your life searching for that special feeling.

I know most of the drug barons who made serious cash from ecstasy and heroin. I used to say fair play to them until I had five young kids with Lila and the streets around our home became full of junkies. It was obvious that something was going to give.

I will always remember 1995 as the year that Dublin was flooded with drugs. The dealers were everywhere. You couldn't walk through Clondalkin without being offered smack by some little bastard.

The drug problem got completely out of control in the estates near my home. If you went to the shops, the first people you met were the dealers. They handed the stuff out for free.

I used to see young kids vomiting on the side of the street after trying heroin for the first time. When I'd meet them a few months later they would be addicts.

'I'm on the gear Bo Bo, you know what I mean?'

It was a nightmare. I thought about what I had done to the kids of the inner city when I worked with Johnson and Larry and Mickey Dunne.

No home in Clondalkin was unaffected. If the junkies were not breaking into my home, they were breaking into my next door neighbours. The young mothers were afraid to let their children out to play on the streets in case they fell on a syringe. Lila was afraid to let our children out. By this stage we had five boys – Lance, Jonathan, Christopher, Jamie and Lee.

The same thing was happening right across the city. I would often visit my friends in the inner city where the drug problem was worse.

I knew one girl who ended up on heroin and she was found dead in the playground with a needle stuck in her right hand.

I knew all about heroin dealing and crime; I knew all the tricks of the trade. Dealers don't think about what they are doing; they think about the money. I always found it hilarious when people used to say on the radio that longer prison sentences deter drug dealers.

Drugs dealers are afraid of no one. When I was selling smack by the kilo I didn't give a fuck about a jail sentence or anything the Minister for Justice had to say. Whether anyone likes to believe it or not, the chances of being caught carrying drugs are nil. And even if you are caught, you can always talk your way out of it. Drug dealing is about money and power.

Addicts don't matter: they are just a source of money. If they don't buy heroin from you, they will buy it somewhere else.

As I said, I had five young children. I was just looking out for myself when a few of the local men in the area came together. They said we all had to do something because the gardaí wouldn't even patrol the estate. The dealers operated everywhere. So we got a bit of a terror campaign going.

When we got together, we decided to slaughter the bastards supplying heroin in the area. The addicts told us who was dealing. To be honest I could have written the list of names even before I made some inquiries.

Our group had a few tough guys. We began by harassing the dealers but they would try to attack back. I remember going on a bus to Ballyfermot and there were about ten of these young guys sitting at the back. They all started shouting at me.

'Come on you viggie! Come on you viggie!'

They called the vigilantes 'viggies'. I didn't look around or say anything but when I went to walk off the bus, they all started stamping their feet on the floor. I started laughing at them.

I got a good look at all their faces. They started to panic when I called them by their names.

'You are like greyhounds when you are in a pack. You are great in a pack, but you are like a little puppy when you are on your own. If I were you, I wouldn't be too fucking smart now.'

They changed their tune when I said I'd see them soon. I tracked every one of them down and knocked the shit out of them.

The whole point of the campaign was to screw them in every way possible. I used to hit the drug pushers for money.

When we would go into a house, that is to kidnap someone, I used to grab the wife or the girlfriend and ask, 'Where's the money he uses to buy the gear?'

I would take the lot. I would take all the money, jewellery or if there was a nice ornament – that was mine. I would take anything that was worth a few quid.

I also pulled a few strokes on dealers. I remember one classic scam where I stole £2,000 on this pusher.

I got 10 ecstasy tablets and went to this drugs pusher in Tallaght. He didn't know I was a vigilante. I asked him if he would be interested in a load.

'How many of them can you get?'

'As many as you want.'

I found these vitamin E tablets. They were identical to these ecstasy tablets they called the white doves. All I had to do was get a nail file and take the numbers off. It took me about three weeks to get vitamins ready for sale. And the stupid dealer fell for it. I did it for the money.

I sold him 5,000 vitamin tablets for £10,000. I gave the money to the Provos, who were now involved in attacking the dealers. But they went mad when they found out where the money came from. Would you believe me if I told you the dealer called me around two weeks later to say the kids were slaughtering the tablets and coming back for more? What could I say?

I sold some fake acid to another dealer. I knew this young fella who could do anything with a computer. I showed him some real acid.

'Could you make something up for me that would look like this?'

I stung a dealer for £20k in cash – for a load of paper embossed with pictures of smiling faces.

The dealer went fucking mad when he realised the consignment was fake.

I just said, 'I don't know anything about it. How the fuck am I supposed to know what acid looks like? I don't take drugs. What do you want me to do?

'I am after buying these tabs from a couple of guys from the North of Ireland and I am only after making £2,000 on the deal. What am I supposed to do?'

Then I would say I was a vigilante. That's how the movement worked. We screwed the pushers. If some teenager owed a big pusher money, our gang would call around and tell the dealer that we stole the money. When we asked them if they wanted the money back, they would say nothing.

When I knocked at the front door of a dealer's house and warned them to stop, I always made sure there were a few strange faces in the crowd with me. This scared the living daylights out of the pushers but it didn't stop them.

I believed we needed to start killing them. In my opinion, it was the only way of stopping the flow of drugs into our area.

You could kick a dealer up and down the road and it would not stop them. As far as I was concerned, a dead dealer couldn't sell drugs.

When the local men and women started patrolling the streets, we started attacking the dealers and threatening to murder them.

I personally abducted about four or five people from their homes in Clondalkin.

I remember dragging one guy kicking and screaming from his bed around 3.00 a.m. or 4.00 a.m. There were five of us involved. I scouted the area for squad cars before we kicked the door of his house down.

The neighbours on both sides knew this was going to happen. They were friends of ours and they had complained about this bastard.

I took a sledgehammer to his door. The locks gave way and we were in. We ran straight upstairs and into his bedroom. He was fast asleep in his bed with his child and this bird. I grabbed the stupid fucker by the throat and spat in his face.

'What do we have here? What a fucking happy family.'

I punched him in the jaw. Another one of the guys whacked him with a baseball bat. He screamed for mercy. Dealers were all the same. They were hard bastards when they were attacking some poor addict; they weren't so hard when they were on their own.

I dragged this particular prick from his bed. He was bawling crying.

We got this guy dressed and took him out. His bird was crying and the baby was screaming. I told his bird that his drug dealing days were over. She grabbed me by the leg and pleaded with me not to kill him. I grabbed her by the hair and bent down.

'What's your fucking problem? You know he's a pusher. Are you not wearing the clothes he buys you? Now get your dirty hands off me you bitch.'

As I walked out the door, I grabbed her once again and said, 'Don't ring the fucking police or we will kill him. Do you understand?'

'I won't.'

I told her if she did, we would be back for her. I told her where her mother lived and said I'd burn the house down.

'Now you know who we are.'

'Are you the IRA?'

'I am not the IRA, but you know who we are. And you know what will happen to you if you open your mouth.'

We dragged him into a van parked around the corner. There was never any danger of these guys going to the gardaí. Even if the gardaí had arrested us there and then, the pushers would have been too afraid to make statements. We were unstoppable.

We took this guy up to the fields near the railway tracks. We battered him and slaughtered him with baseball bats. I kicked that bastard in the head so hard that I knocked two of his teeth out.

When he could take no more, I doused him with petrol. I wanted to set him on fire but the others wouldn't let me. I did the same thing to a few dealers. One guy was called Simon Doyle. He was shot dead a year later in a gangland feud. Everyone blamed his murder on me. I didn't give a fuck. I was glad that everyone thought I had plugged that fucker. He was a little bastard. I hope he's rotting in hell. He was just a prick. We could have wiped him out but someone else did it first.

The people took the law into their own hands right across the city. Anti-drugs committees were established in every community. The local people came together and started marching on the homes of the big dealers. The vigilantes stayed away from the committees because we were kicking doors in.

They would hold meetings where they would summons the local dealers to come and make a confession. The newspapers called these meetings 'kangaroo courts' but they worked. The anti-drugs movement wanted to show the children just how scared the dealers were of the community.

Sinn Féin and the Provos joined the street movement when they realised the level of community support the marches attracted but they were only interested in a few votes.

I used to go on a few marches but I was more interested in taking direct action against the dealers. As far as I was concerned, you could march on their homes all you wanted, but it would do no good. I knew what the dealers needed. I had no time for standing around talking shop.

I got together with a few locals guys and decided to take direct action against the pushers. The people on the committees knew nothing about this gang. They wanted to clean up the streets through peaceful means and through showing the drug dealers the damage they were doing to their areas, whereas I wanted to murder and intimidate the pushers.

The IRA always took credit for clearing heroin dealers from the estates around Dublin but they didn't. It was the local men who did the real dirty work. I have to admit, though, that a few members of the IRA did help out in a personal capacity.

Some of the guys in the Provos and Sinn Féin were genuine but others were just there to get votes. The genuine guys wanted to start assassinating the dealers but the IRA leadership always stopped them, although the boys did assassinate a few of them. The Provos shot P.J. Judge, who was one of the biggest heroin importers in Dublin. The same IRA crew also shot the drug dealer Joe Foran in Finglas and Thomas Reilly in Rathfarnham. I believe Foran was shot by a Provo. There was a queue of them offering to do the hit. The guy just fired a single bullet into his head while he sat in a car with his girlfriend. I hope the fucker choked to death.

Unfortunately the IRA in Clondalkin was all talk and no action. When I wanted to kill the local pushers they wouldn't let me. The dealers even felt confident enough to come to us and have informal talks.

I was present and a few of them made statements. They would give us the names of people involved in smuggling drugs to get themselves out of trouble.

There was one guy who did this the whole time. His name was Declan Griffin and he lived around the corner from my home.

Griffin was arrested at Dublin airport with millions of pounds worth of heroin. When he was charged he claimed he was working for the gardaí. Griffin told just about anyone who would listen that he was an informer. The local IRA boys and a few of us kidnapped him to find out exactly what was going on.

We took Griffin into the Dublin mountains and kicked the shit out of him. We tied him up and placed him in a hole for three days. He cried like a baby. He begged us to let him go the first day but we didn't. I put tape over his mouth and placed a pillowcase over his head. We left him there until he started telling the truth.

Griffin had poisoned hundreds of children. I wanted to kill him and bury his body but the IRA wouldn't allow me. They wanted him alive. At the time, Griffin was facing charges and they wanted to see what he would say in court about his work as an informer. This is exactly what the IRA was about.

I believe the attacks on the drug dealers worked. We frightened them; they found it difficult to operate in Clondalkin because they didn't know who would be kidnapped or shot next.

The campaign to clear the streets worked because we had one simple rule. If a drug dealer threatened or attacked one of us; we would take revenge. No matter what a drug dealer did, they knew that if one of our men was even intimidated, they would be shot dead.

You might ask if I regret becoming a vigilante. You could even call me a hypocrite because I was once a drug dealer, but I don't regret it for a second. I'm just sorry I didn't kill a few pushers. But I am glad that the Provos whacked a few of them. My only regret is that the Provos didn't kill a few more.

chapter sixteen

Life has a strange way of knocking you for six when you least expect it. My life was turned upside down in 1997 when some victims of the religious orders went public with their stories. I can still remember the first time I heard a news bulletin announcing to the world that the gardaí were running investigations into sex abuse in several industrial schools. I was drinking a cup of tea when I heard the news. I have to admit that I froze.

I convinced myself the investigations would go nowhere but I was wrong. When the victims started telling their stories to the newspapers, they opened up a can of worms. It was like an avalanche. The government and the religious orders found themselves on the run.

I became one of the men who came forward to tell our stories.

I joined a group called the Irish Survivors of Child Abuse. We started holding small meetings at first in the Ashling Hotel in Dublin. Seven or eight men would come and we would argue about how we should start a campaign for justice.

I threw myself into SOCA because I had plenty of time on my hands. The anti-drugs movement had wound up. I would spend my days making phone calls and contacting people asking them for help. I worked alongside a man called John Kelly. He became my hero. I had never met anyone who worked so hard for others.

The SOCA campaign brought back the memories of the abuse. I began to have nightmares and panic attacks when I went to sleep. But the nightmares were worth it.

A team of detectives from Bandon in County Cork eventually contacted me. They asked me to make a written statement about my abusers. It took me 14 hours to put everything down in words. Nobody was charged with any criminal offence because Br. Buglar and the rest of the men that abused us had long since died. But I can say the victims are still glad we made our statements; it helped us to erase some troubles from our minds. I genuinely appreciate the work the gardaí did to investigate my claims.

It was funny really. I spent my whole life fighting with the gardaí but the detectives on the inquiry showed me great kindness. I still call them occasionally to say hello.

I have now gone full circle. I suppose you could say I am going around the second time. I feel like a new man. Believe it or not, I have now left crime behind me. Even if I wanted to do a bit of business on the side, I couldn't because I have a heart condition and don't have the time. There is much work to be done for SOCA and I don't know how long I have left in life.

I still have a lot of flashbacks. I've been going to a professional therapist called Muriel Moran for the past couple of years. She's brought a lot of my past life to the surface. I'm now at the stage where I remember everything. She tells me that my emotional feelings are now back in some sort of order. You may not think I'm in good emotional order but you would agree with her if you met me 20 years ago.

When I think back on my life I wonder if things could have been different. I never once owned a bank account but I have lived like a lord. I was never really short of money. I always had a few quid and I always dressed well.

But I never wanted to be that type of guy. My mother and father never wanted me to be that type of guy. They only wanted me to receive a bit of education that could see me through life. They are both dead now. Da died in 1976 and Ma passed away three years ago.

I am truly sorry for what I did. I wish I could start out again. I have hurt those who mattered the most to me. I have hurt my children. I destroyed my first family and hurt my friend Lobbins. She never deserved the life I gave her. I only hope that she can learn to forgive me. I ask the same of Lila who I have also hurt.

I hope my children never end up like me. I hope they don't waste their lives. I hope they will learn from my mistakes. I hope they become good people and live normal lives.

I have only one photograph of myself as a child. It was taken in Upton. I look as if I have the whole world in front of me. I often look at that picture and wish I could go back in time and become that 12-year-old boy again. If I could I would do everything so differently. If I could go back in time, I would get a job, work hard and do the right thing by my family. I never wanted to be the animal that came out of Upton. I never wanted to be a bad father even though I was. I am still trying to discover why I did what I did but my only hope is that my children know they mean the world to me even if I always didn't show it. I am writing this book for them – to help them understand why I am the person I am. I just hope I succeeded.